CULTURE SHOCK!

Havana
At your Door

Mark Cramer

Graphic Arts Center Publishing Company
Portland, Oregon

In the same series

Argentina	*Egypt*	*Korea*	*Spain*
Australia	*Finland*	*Laos*	*Sri Lanka*
Austria	*France*	*Malaysia*	*Sweden*
Bolivia	*Germany*	*Mauritius*	*Switzerland*
Borneo	*Greece*	*Mexico*	*Syria*
Britain	*Hong Kong*	*Morocco*	*Taiwan*
Burma	*Hungary*	*Myanmar*	*Thailand*
California	*India*	*Nepal*	*Turkey*
Canada	*Indonesia*	*Netherlands*	*UAE*
Chile	*Iran*	*Norway*	*Ukraine*
China	*Ireland*	*Pakistan*	*USA*
Cuba	*Israel*	*Philippines*	*USA—The South*
Czech Republic	*Italy*	*Singapore*	*Venezuela*
Denmark	*Japan*	*South Africa*	*Vietnam*

Barcelona At Your Door	*Paris At Your Door*	*A Wife's Guide*
Chicago At Your Door	*Rome At Your Door*	*Living and Working*
Havana At Your Door	*San Francisco At Your Door*	*Abroad*
Jakarta At Your Door		*Working Holidays*
Kuala Lumpur, Malaysia	*A Globe-Trotter's Guide*	*Abroad*
At Your Door	*A Parent's Guide*	
London At Your Door	*A Student's Guide*	
New York At Your Door	*A Traveller's Medical Guide*	

Illustrations by TRIGG
Front cover photograph by Liba Taylor
Back cover photograph by International Photobank
Inside photographs by Mark Cramer unless otherwise stated

© 2000 Times Media Private Limited
Reprinted 2001

This book is published by special
arrangement with Times Media Private Limited
Times Centre, 1 New Industrial Road, Singapore 536196
International Standard Book Number 1-55868-531-6
Library of Congress Catalog Number 99-65772
Graphic Arts Center Publishing Company
P.O. Box 10306 • Portland, Oregon 97296-0306 • (503) 226-
2402

Printed in Singapore

To Jonathan Griffiths,
who, like Elegguá, pointed the way.

CONTENTS

ACKNOWLEDGEMENTS

My thanks to editor Kenneth Chang for his genuine interest in the subject, Trigg for his sly way of capturing the message, Tomás Burgos for his poems and other insights, my brother Fred for finding me the right computer, hundreds of Cubans who made me feel at home and shared their ideas with great warmth and generosity, and my partner Martha Sonia for her critical readings and moral support.

INTRODUCTION

Whenever I write about Cuba, I receive knee-jerk lectures from people who have never been there (usually U.S. acquaintances). These lectures attempt to put me on the defensive, as if I were an official of the Cuban government or an evil defender of dictatorships. Curiously, these same people have no objections when I've written about Mexico, a country whose population has endured a seven-decade, one-party dictatorship with an infamous record of police abuse, hordes of desperate refugees exiting the country, and periodic quasi-official massacres of its own citizens — usually poor Indian peasants, students, and independent journalists.

The same critics who instinctively put me on the defensive about Cuba are not bothered when I write about Bolivia, where 70 percent of the population lives in abject poverty, a country whose corrupt officialdom belongs to a plutocracy (with no real opposition) that has lacked the will to take any courageous measures that would improve the country's embarrassing record in terms of literacy, life expectancy, infant mortality, environmental issues, and general quality of life.

I can only guess that the double standard of my critics regarding Cuba has something to do with either self-censorship or succumbing to the effects of a sophisticated consciousness industry that has caused them to accept prepackaged clichés about this extraordinarily exciting country. I, too, was once prone to simplistic stereotypes about Cuba. But then a visionary editor at Times Media, Jonathan Griffiths, suggested that I go there and do a book called *Culture Shock! Cuba*. Since my first stay in Cuba, my life has forever changed its course, with a Before and After Cuba — B.C. and A.C.

The city of Havana has become a magnet for thousands of repeat-visit travelers from around the world, including this writer, who can't absorb enough with one or two stays. But many good people who would otherwise immediately fall in love with the place are deterred from going there by the dominant media platitudes.

Havana has all the traits of a great tourist site: superb beaches, participatory and spectator sports, tropical warmth, a rich history, and a dynamic culture. But Havana has much more. It is the only Latin American capital (and one of the few in the world) whose colonial architectures have not been disrupted by modern utilitarian building projects. Havana resounds with a lively and contagious music scene, highlighted by great Afro-Cuban genres like rumba, salsa, and *son*, which strike their rhythmic chords throughout the world. The city has a fascinating religious culture dominated by Santería, a hybrid of Catholic and West African religious traditions. It has the best cigars in the world, and many would argue the best coffee as well. And above all, Havana has its people — for the most part a racially-harmonious blend of peoples of African and Spanish descent, whose friendliness is legendary.

Whether you plan to come here or not, don't let the prevailing propaganda dissuade you from finding out more about this great city. Within these pages, listen to what Habaneros of all backgrounds and persuasions have to say, get a feel for the city's lively street-life and joyous public gathering places, experience the dramatic struggle of a cultured people to overcome what seem to be insurmountable obstacles, and confront the bittersweet contradictions of an idiosyncratic urban setting with little resemblance to any other city in the world.

HAVANA
by Tomás Burgos

Rumba dancing, gothic mulata,
Havana, flashing darkly in the clear sunlight
colossal rock in the Gulf,
raucous and capricious,
your night disappears where the bay meets the sea.
Havana, immense city, so small
you fit in the luggage of your children,
so deep you never end,
complicated and simple,
a Caribbean flower is a slice of your air,
borderless encounters,
unconditional embrace,
the wayfarers' muse,
Havana ancient and new,
a city conjured up,
unpredictable, fiery, aphrodisian,
phoenix bird surging from the shadows,
agile remedy for all catastrophes,
cobblestone, congas and castanet,
baroque, neoclassic and Arabesque,
Capital of brightness,
confluence of two waters
shimmering at the island portal
rejuvenated long ago
swaying to bolero and guaguancó.

CHAPTER ONE

PHYSICAL SETTING:
The Quirky City

PICTURE IT . . .

Centro Habana is a funky neighborhood with colonial buildings in disrepair lining narrow streets. Here and there, buildings are being restored . Wrecking crews deal with hopeless cases. Blueprints approximating colonial designs await financing. Clothing drapes to dry over intricate balconies that deserve to be featured in museums of colonial architecture. And within, dark corridors lead to asymmetrical interiors whose infrastructural inadequacies are sometimes compensated for with creative, makeshift solutions.

People (mostly black but also white and mulatto) are hanging out in the street, chatting, swigging beer, sipping coffee, sitting on stoops or standing on corners. Pedestrians walk in the middle of the pavement, veering to the sidewalk to avoid an occasional vintage American automobile from the 1940s or 1950s. Children play stickball with makeshift bats, remarkably reminiscent of the grittier streets of New York City.

I was walking through these streets one Sunday when I heard the complex, layered rhythms of rumba music coming from an open inner patio. I edged closer to the music. Two Afro-Cuban women and one man with dreadlocks welcomed me in. The taller of the two women, wearing overalls that reminded me of the Mississippi Delta, explained that the ceremony commemorated the restoration of their apartment building, which had housed 36 families until the infrastructure had become a serious safety hazard. A Canadian-Cuban consortium had decided to restore the building, and tenants were moved to temporary housing.

The three rumba drummers, soaring with the music, were surrounded by admiring listeners who broke out in choral accompaniment. Beneath the sacred ceiba tree in the center patio were food offerings (part of a Santerían ritual) including pineapples, which I had not been able to find at the produce market because they were out of season. When it was time to dance around the tree in a procession, the two women grabbed me by my arms and guided me around. A Japanese tourist had been siphoned into the patio by the rumba contagion and was snapping photos. Following the dance, a young man stood up facing the tree chanting words in Yoruban, a West African language.

I was later told that the inhabitants were moving back into the building. Unlike costly restoration projects I'd seen in other countries, this one did not price out the original tenants. They were returning with the same rent: one tenth of their monthly salary, which for some meant as little as two dollars.

My greatest surprise was kept for last. I was told that this building was where Cuban musical great Chano Pozo had been born. During the bebop era of the late 1940s and early 1950s, Chano, a follower of the Afro-Cuban Abakuá cult, had been hired by Dizzy Gillespie to teach his drummers Afro-Cuban rhythms. The immediate result was a musical genre called cubop. Chano's indelible imprint remains within the rhythms of the contemporary jazz scene.

This experience is just a glimpse of the massive restoration project going on today in colonial Old Havana (bordering the harbor) and spreading out into Centro Habana and along the Malecón boulevard overlooking the north coast of the city. In the history of urban restoration, nothing approaches either the magnitude or the human compassion of Havana's ongoing architectural renaissance.

A trio of conga players celebrates the restoration of Chano Pozo's birthplace.

A DIFFERENT HISTORY FROM THE REST

The Spanish Crown's "Laws of the Indies" should have traditionally imposed a straight, grid-like street design upon Havana's oldest quarter, founded in 1519 and now known as **Old Havana** (Habana Vieja). Instead, narrow, intimate streets emerged, at times curving to fit the pattern of Havana Bay, which surrounds the city on three sides. This irregular grid is interrupted by five main squares (each lined with various churches and palatial structures), all of which survive today: **Plaza de la Catedral, Plaza Nueva** (today called Plaza Vieja), **Plaza de San Francisco, Plaza de Cristo**, and **Plaza de Armas**. Numerous smaller and more intimate squares also adorn the quarter. The residential streets and neighborhoods winding around these plazas are no less impressive; you'll find intricate stone masonry, wrought-iron or wood balconies, shaded porticoes, high windows with sculpted stone moldings, imposing doorways, and stained glass windows.

Old Havana was originally protected by a rampart (small sections of which survive today) and a series of stone fortresses (which now function as museums), intended as a line of defense against pirate raids. The most famous of these fortresses, just across the narrow entryway to Havana Bay, is the **Castillo del Morro**, built between 1589 and 1630. It remains well-preserved today and is brilliantly illuminated during the night. From El Morro, the view of the city across the bay is nothing less than spectacular, especially at sunset.

By the seventeenth century, the Old Quarter had spread out westward beyond its rampart. Havana gets younger as it extends west—architectural testimony of its stages of development. **Centro Habana**, the second stage of the city's development, maintained the same narrow, residential streets, although commercial corridors were wider than in the Old Quarter. By the nineteenth century, the population outside the rampart exceeded the intramural population, and the walls were rendered useless. In their place,

15

Straits
of
Florida

MALECÓN

Máximo Gómez
monument

Canal del Puerto

PASEO DEL PRADO

AVE DE LAS MISIONES

Museo de la
Revolución

Bellas
Artes

EMPEDRADO

12

1

2

Museo de Arte
Colonial

OBISPO

OBRAPÍA

Gran Teatro
de La
Habana

6

10

16

3

5

BRASIL

4

Capitolio

VILLEGAS

9

15

EGIDO

8

14

7

11

13

Museo Casa Natal de
José Martí

Havana Bay

Outdoor Gathering Places in Old Havana

1.-Plaza de la Catedral
2.-Plaza de Armas
3.-Plaza de
  San Francisco
4.-Plaza Vieja
5.-Plaza del Cristo
6.-Parque Central

7.-Plazuela de la Luz
8.-Plazoleta de Belen
9.-Plazoleta de las
  Ursulinas
10.-Plazoleta de Albear
11.-Estación Central
  (railroad terminal)

12.-Maestranza
13.-Plazuela de Paula
14.-Plazoleta del
  Espiritu Santo
15.-Plazuela de
  Santa Clara
16.-Plazuela de san
  Fco. el Nuevo

16

the city had been slowly developing a network of parks, including **Parque Central**, **Parque de la Fraternidad**, and **Parque de los Enamorados** (Lover's Park, near the oceanfront), as well as a wooded walkway with embedded stone benches and a sculpted stone barrier separating two lanes of carriage traffic (forming a neat line between the inner Old Havana and the then outer Centro Habana). The walkway, today known as **Paseo del Prado** or **Paseo Martí**, resembles Barcelona's Las Ramblas. El Prado had been developing in stages since the late 1700s. A few blocks to the south, the enormous ceiba tree in Parque de la Fraternidad was nourished with earth brought in from all the Americas.

A restored building in Old Havana.

17

Sunset view of Havana from El Morro.

The rampart began to come down in 1863, but today a few attractive remnants of it still stand. Larger quadrants allowed for the construction of more majestic buildings, including what are now the Inglaterra and Plaza hotels. In the same area just outside the former wall, old tobacco factories remain as splendid living relics of industrial architecture. You can tour these factories, whether your interest is in cigars or urban history.

Styles of architecture in and around the "newer" area of El Prado include art deco (e.g., the Bacardi office building), Arabic-influenced buildings with patterned facades and arched windows, and neoclassical structures (e.g., the Capitolio, with its great dome). By the end of the nineteenth century, residential housing in El Prado and the Old Quarter began to decline as Havana's version of "white flight" led to newer communities farther west, exemplified by El Vedado. Former palaces in the older quarters were divided into rental flats, with communal bathrooms added haphazardly, usually in courtyards, resembling in design the *vecindades* in the historic center of Mexico City.

With Old Havana touching the harbor on three sides, many first floors of residential buildings were converted into shipping warehouses. The shops along Obispo Street, a must-see and a must-stroll for today's visitor, developed within historic buildings during the port boom of the early 1900s. A financial sector known as "Little Wall Street" also emerged within Old Havana during this period.

Nearly a quarter of the 4,000 buildings in today's Old Havana have a high heritage value. Other buildings — no less quaint in character — can be seen with the ubiquitous clothing draped to dry over beautiful balconies. Repetition of such imagery is more a question of urban patterns than redundancy.

Havana and the Revolution

A common belief is that the Old Quarter began to decline after the 1959 revolution, but decay in this sector dates to the time, decades earlier, when the creole elite had fled west. Decay escalated when the post-1959 revolutionary government virtually abandoned the city in order to spend its meager resources on uplifting the countryside. But this policy, apparently negative for Havana, actually achieved two positive results:

1. The core of the city remained heterogeneous. Unlike every other Latin American capital, Havana did not experience the thoughtless, anti-historical building boom of the 1960s and beyond. Whole historical blocks and sectors were not razed in the name of "urban renewal."

2. By investing first and foremost in rural areas and smaller cities, Cuba averted the dramatic phenomenon typical of other Latin American capitals: the massive influx of unskilled peasants to the city and the subsequent development of a socially marginal underclass living in makeshift hovels.

19

The Special Period

In theory, the costly renovation of the Old Quarter should have proceeded evenly since UNESCO officially recognized Havana's historic center as a World Heritage Site. But with the loss of Soviet economic support by 1990 and the subsequent escalation of the U.S. embargo ("the Blockade" according to most Cubans), Havana and the rest of Cuba went through what was labeled "the Special Period in a time of peace." With no opportunity for commerce with the city's nearest and natural trading partner 90 miles to the north, and with the loss of its main source of spare parts, fuel, and imported foods, Cuba fell into a deep depression. Havana's infrastructure was at the point of no return, and no observer remained unmoved by the eerie urban landscape resembling a bombed-out city.

For those of us who observed the "before" of the mid-1990s and the "after" at the turn of the century, the ongoing massive renovation of Old Havana, Centro Habana, and many of the sea-salt-damaged buildings lining the Malecón seawall is nothing short of miraculous. Most cities around the world, when confronted with the steeper costs of restoration as opposed to gutting and rebuilding, chose the latter, thus losing many of their most artistic and historic buildings to urban renewal. In such cities, outdoor museum pieces are replaced by utilitarian office structures, with the city's architectural and historical unity lost forever. Havana has boldly chosen the most difficult path: renovation whenever it is technically possible, no matter what the cost. The initial costs are difficult to absorb, but the long-term investment with such a strategy has both tangible and intangible benefits in the realms of tourism and quality of life.

Funding has come from a combination of foreign investment and dividends from Cuba's rapidly escalating tourism industry. As we shall see, such progress has not been without its down side. The parallel dollar economy (required by the tourist industry and a Cuban treasury in need of hard currency) has created social inequalities unknown since 1959. Half of the Cuban population now receives dollars in the form of tips from tourists or gifts from Cuban exiles, while the other half does not. Since most exiles are whites, more white Cubans receive dollars than black Cubans. Several Cubans complained to this writer that foreign companies are not always as willing as the Cuban government has been to employ blacks on an equal basis. Many blacks who once unequivocally supported Fidel Castro are now among the disgruntled. Ironically, Castro had opposed the parallel dollar economy but was overruled by the Central Committee of the Communist Party.

Nevertheless, were it not for the growth of tourism, the crumbling infrastructure of historic Havana may not have been saved, and Cuba may have succumbed to the effects of the trade embargo.

CITY PLANNING

Under the humane guidance of **Eusebio Leal Spengler**, Historian of the City of Havana, the renovation of Havana's extensive historic districts is proceeding with a keen awareness of potential

21

social problems associated with gentrification, as reflected in other countries. Leal and his city planners are conscious of the danger of displacing residential sectors by service sectors, the negative impacts of the uncontrolled development of tourism, and the increase of vehicular traffic.

The great human and aesthetic drama of the restoration of historic Havana is one exciting reason for visiting the city precisely at this time. "Before-and-after" photographers must hurry in before it is too late. When the temporarily displaced residents of Chano Pozo's old apartment building in Centro Habana were welcomed back, it was a historic example of city planners averting gentrification. Previous examples of urban renewal around the world show whole populations priced out of their old neighborhood, as this writer observed in the Twentieth Arrondissement of Paris and in the SoHo neighborhood of Manhattan.

Before and after at the Malecón.

Planning maps reflecting Mr. Leal's vision of restoration show areas marked R (for "residential") integrated within the plan, thus protecting the mixed-use nature of Old Havana. The contrary approach would be to force residents out of commercially valuable sectors, creating the type of all-commerce district that has effectively destroyed the street life of many modern urban settings. The Havana planners have opted for the protection of street-life by keeping residence and commerce in cozy proximity. This mixed-use philosophy shows no signs of faltering. In "before-and-after" stays in Havana, I found the same colorful "neighborhood characters" in front of renovated buildings. Street-life in Havana's living historic sectors is as vibrant as ever.

Unplanned Benefits: When "Bad" Leads To Good

Apparently negative scenarios have paved the way for positive outcomes. Some of these twists in destiny are here noted:

1. Conventional wisdom suggests that developers are essential for the well-being of cities. But the absence of development in Havana led to a positive result: the saving of historic Havana from the wrecking ball of unprincipled speculation. Coincidentally, the near total abandonment of the city occurred during a period when the world was hardly conscious of the value of historical preservation. Havana slept through a "world war" against cities and woke up precisely when the world desired to make architectural peace with its past.

2. No one wants a fuel shortage, but in Havana, during the scariest moments of the "Special Period," after Cuba had suddenly lost 40 percent of her foreign trade (including her primary fuel sources), Fidel proclaimed the "era of the bicycle." More than a million Chinese bicycles were distributed throughout the country, and Havana was spared the grievous pollution problems that now plague car-dominated Latin American capitals like Mexico City and Santiago, Chile.

3. By most economic indicators, Havana was totally lacking in large-scale, capital-intensive commerce. Result: the urban setting is not scarred by Golden Arches, billboards, and neon signs. Smaller, more picturesque, and more informal businesses add considerable spice to street-life.

4. A vast majority of Havana residents are apartment dwellers. The average of 1.9 persons per bedroom in the Old Quarter is not overcrowded by Latin American standards, but would be considered cramped by Westerners who do not live in Paris or Manhattan. With this type of housing density, the street becomes an extension of the home, and public gathering places thrive. The street becomes a community living room.

EAST-TO-WEST NEIGHBORHOOD TOUR

Havana's social, commercial, and political life revolves around one's community. As shall be repeated for emphasis, the best strategy for the newcomer to become integrated with the city's rhythms and flavors is to hang out in the same neighborhood. An encyclopedic approach to getting to know this city (by hopping around from one neighborhood to another) is contrary to Havana's social logic. Even a short-stay visitor would do well to use a single neighborhood as a base for most social activities and commerce. After a short time, one feels attached to the city for having gotten to know the neighbors and having made friends.

A brief description of Havana's most important neighborhoods will serve as a gauge with which the future visitor can make a choice of temporary or long-term residence. Whenever my personal persuasions intervene, it shall be dutifully noted.

Old Havana

This city began right here, surrounded on three sides by a deep harbor. With so many attractions, this is the must neighborhood for every visitor. Spending time in any of the five main plazas,

Plaza in Old Havana.

especially **Plaza de la Catedral** and **Plaza de Armas**, browsing for new and used books at outdoor stands, entering art galleries, listening to music genres like *son*, boleros, salsa, rumba, *trova*, or Latin jazz emanating from different restaurants and outdoor bandstands, visiting the interiors of historic buildings (many of which have been converted into quirky museums), drinking a *mojito* in an elegant colonial tourist trap, shopping at Obispo street boutiques—these are a few of the daily and nightly pleasures of Old Havana.

For this writer, the greatest attractions of Old Havana are its residential streets. Amazingly, within a few paces of upscale tourist attractions, such as Hemingway's favorite bar, **La Bodeguita del Medio** (on Empedrado), one can find ancient residential dwellings inhabited by proletarian Havana residents. In any other "old town" in the world, working class inhabitants would have long since been priced out of the neighborhood. This mix of upscale and working class is unbeatable for keeping a community dynamic. A comparable mix may be found in the Adams-Morgan neighborhood in Washington, D.C., the Mission District in San Francisco, the West Village in Manhattan, and the Twentieth Arrondissement in Paris.

The presence of these grungy residential streets may save Old Havana from evolving into a type of "Disneyland of Cuban Culture."

Centro Habana

I make this district my personal choice as a place to stay when I'm in Havana. Readers can decide whether or not they identify with my criteria. The streets of Centro Habana, usually as intimately narrow as those of Old Havana, are grittier and feel more African. The architecture is generally newer than that of Old Havana but it still dates back to the colonial era, with a dazzling variety of intricate facades and balconies.

Strategically this neighborhood is within walking distance of **Parque de la Fraternidad** and **Parque Central** (center), the cigar factories (center), the Malecón promenade (north), store and street shopping (center and west), Chinatown (center-west), Old Havana (east), the train station (south), and the bus station (west, if you have good legs). I've also walked from this district to contiguous neighborhoods like Vedado and Cerro, and to the ferry in Old Havana that takes you to Regla.

Chinatown offers a surprising change of pace from the routine Cuban diet (at very reasonable prices and with roving musicians serenading *son* and bolero). At the **Malecón**, a long seawall, one can spend hours soaking in the ocean breeze, chatting, fishing, or even jumping into the water with the neighborhood children. In the heart of the district are produce market bargains within the peso economy, a fresh and healthy diet for visitors who prefer to self-cater. Perhaps the neighborhood's greatest attraction is its considerable population of believers in Santería (the most dominant sect of Afro-Cuban religion which syncretizes African saints with their Catholic equivalents). People dressed in white from hat to shoes are in their first year of Santería instruction. Rumba rumbles through the streets.

27

Small food stands dealing in national currency offer rich Cuban coffee for a peso (about US$0.04), a slice of pizza for 5 or 6 pesos, and on main streets, delicious Cuban ice cream, any brand of which is of gourmet quality.

At the northwest edge of Centro Habana, just before Vedado, the unusual community of **Cayo Hueso** is painstakingly restoring its early twentieth-century tenements with the participation of the residents themselves. Afro-Cuban murals highlight the neighborhood's Santería tradition, and narrow alleys lend it an intimate feeling.

Under the current system, the great neighborhoods in Centro Habana will never become gentrified. But should a new system usher in a money-driven housing market, a middle class might move in and this neighborhood would be in danger of losing some degree of its funky charm.

A gritty street in Centro Habana.

Vedado

Vedado lies to the west of Centro Habana, which means it is newer. The general tone of the architecture is pretty generic, symbolized by its numbered and lettered avenues and streets. If Cuba were to have a class structure, then Vedado would be a middle-class neighborhood. Vedado's history has had its ups and downs. It was once the new home of the creole elite after they evacuated Old Havana, but the same elite eventually moved farther west to create a more elegant district called Miramar. Today, Vedado comes alive as a center of culture and university life.

The district has more than a few nooks and crannies of interest. Vedado's grand old **Hotel Nacional de Cuba** (northeast), a vestige from Batista and crime-syndicate times, is a landmark towering over the Malecón. Aesthetically, **La Plaza de la Revolución** is not nearly as attractive as its Old Havana counterparts, but the Pope came here, and the Che Guevara mural must be seen. The **University of Havana** is also located in Vedado, so foreign students coming to Cuba may find it strategic to obtain an apartment or homestay here. Vedado also contains Havana's version of an off-Broadway theater district.

Vedado's most distinct attraction may be the **Cementerio de Colón** (southwest), with its funerary sculptures and historic "residents." Strategically, it's a fairly long but pleasant walk east along the Malecón from Vedado to Centro and Old Havana, and the bus station is just north of the Plaza de la Revolución.

Vedado's sense of place is enhanced by the city block occupied by the **Coppelia** ice cream palace, set under a canopy of trees and one of Havana's great public gathering places. Scenes from the prize-winning film, *Fresa y Chocolate* (Strawberry and Chocolate) were filmed at this location (the largest Coppelia outlet in Cuba). The finale of another award-winning film, *Guantanamera*, takes place in the cemetery. Rent these two films before you go to Havana and see some of the Vedado district.

Miramar

You get from Vedado to Miramar by traveling west through tunnels under the Almendares River. Miramar's main thoroughfare, **Quinta Avenida** (Fifth Avenue), shows off a luxuriant garden in its center boulevard, and is lined on both sides by former mansions and shade trees, including the *jaguey* (banyan tree), whose roots destroy all nearby vegetation, but whose extensive shade is Havana's best natural air conditioner on humid summer days.

After the revolution, Miramar's luxury mansions were converted into government office buildings or fractioned into housing. The presence of foreign missions makes this district an "embassy row." Here and there, an abandoned villa remains as a relic of the fall of Batista. Compared to the Malecón, Miramar's sea front offers more privacy and less grittiness.

The **Maqueta de la Ciudad** is one of Miramar's important features. This is an impressive scale model of the city of Havana. Go west on Fifth Avenue as the cross-street numbers rise from 1 to 42. At 28th Street, turn right for a block-and-a-half, just short of the ocean. Miramar's other landmark is the **Cira García International Clinic**, an important symbol of Cuba's health tourism, to the southeast of the district.

From Parque de la Fraternidad, suburban Miramar is reached by intermittent bus service, about a 9 mile (14 km) ride. Miramar is pretty, but too spread out for the type of cohesive community life one finds in most Havana neighborhoods.

OTHER NEIGHBORHOODS

Pre-1959 suburban development spread west of Miramar to woodsier areas like Siboney. On our east-to-west neighborhood tour, we traveled parallel to Malecón, with the sea to our right. Now let's move inland and circle back from west to east. Each of the neighborhoods we pass through will be south of the coast until we reach Playas del Este on the beach.

Marianao

South of Miramar is Marianao, whose **Tropicana** nightclub is the rejuvenating grandmother of the Havana club scene. For those who can't handle a cover charge which amounts to about three months of an average Cuban's salary, you'll find other music-and-dance spectacles for considerably less. (See Chapter 9.)

Cerro

South of Vedado is the fascinating Cerro district, whose primary landmark is the **Estadio Latinoamericano**, the setting for the drama of Havana's baseball league. (The season lasts from November through March.) **Tip!** Baseball is Cuba's national sport and a primary conversation topic as the season heads for the March playoffs; even if you've never understood the sport, give it a try.

Beyond the stadium, Cerro has the look of a middle-class Latin American suburb, becoming less attractive in its southernmost section. Small segments within Cerro (which you'll never see if you remain on primary avenues) contain the type of makeshift hovels more typical of extensive slums in other Latin American capitals. Havana dwellers refer to the residents of these communities as "Palestinians"—rural Cubans who are officially discouraged from migrating to the big city.

Havana suffers considerably less from this type of urban squalor because the post-1959 government went against the Latin American grain and put the larger part of its resources into rural Cuba, thus preventing the massive rural-to-urban migration that has plagued cities like Mexico City or Lima, Peru. Cubans appalled by the living conditions of the so-called "Palestinians" might be surprised to observe the vast *ciudades perdidas* in Mexico City, the *favelas* in Rio de Janeiro, the *barriadas* in Lima, or the *laderas* in La Paz, Bolivia. Cubans have less toleration for this sort of thing because they were told by their leaders that it is unacceptable.

Notwithstanding such ramshackle nooks, Cerro is mainly a quiet, residential neighborhood.

31

An ornate facade in Regla.

Regla and Guanabacoa

Continuing east, past the south end of the bay, we arrive in Regla, which is also reached by ferry from Old Havana. Regla is one of Havana's many communities with strong Santería roots, as is neighboring Guanabacoa. Both Regla and Guanabacoa have attractive colonial centers with industrial outskirts. Each has a local museum with eclectic collections of Afro-Cuban cultural relics. In Regla, there is the **Museo Municipal de Regla**; in Guanabacoa, the **Museo Histórico de Guanabacoa**.

Playas del Este

These "east beaches," about 12 miles (20 km) from Havana, are reached through the Havana Bay tunnel or by alternate roads splitting between Regla and Guanabacoa. Tourist guides map out Playas del Este as a single place, but in reality it has a split personality. On the west segment (the side nearer to Havana) are the beach resort venues of **El Megano** and **Santa María del Mar**, which most Cubans from Havana feel are off-limits to them. Here is a good place to visit Cuba without mixing with any Cubans other than waiters, bellboys, receptionists, invited entertainers, and a few clever hustlers.

On the east side of Playas del Este are communities converging around **Guanabo**, a real Cuban town. The beaches seem less manicured, with a few soft, white exceptions around **Boca Ciega**. The hotels are less touristy but comfortable, and Guanabo even has homestay opportunities and homespun *paladar* alternatives to the rather unsensational but more expensive restaurants on the resort side of Playas del Este.

A Few Other Districts . . .

In the vicinity of the Havana international airport (southwest) are the spread-out districts of **Boyeros**, with an **Expocuba** exhibit and the **Parque Lenin** complex, and **Arroyo Naranjo**, a botanical garden with an organic restaurant and exhibits on Cuba's successful experiments in organic agriculture.

Dull, block-like post-revolutionary housing projects can be seen east of the bay in the vicinity of **Alamar**.

GEOGRAPHIC SETTING

Havana is a largely flat city, with suburban areas on three sides (west, south, east) and the Straits of Florida to the north. Its natural bay, between Old Havana and East Havana, opens up into four mini-bays, called *ensenadas*, like a thin wrist and larger hand opening up into four stubby fingers.

Climate

This is a tropical city with mild and comfortable weather for much of the year but a steamy summer from June through September. During the mild winter, a windbreaker or blazer may be necessary. Visitors sensitive to the blast of air conditioning in some restaurants and hotel lobbies may need to keep a jacket handy even in warmer months. The mean annual temperature is 79°F (26°C). This drops to 73°F (23°C) in January and rises to 82°F (28°C) in August, the hottest month, when highs are above 90°F (32°C) and the humidity is an offender of human rights.

Plants and Wildlife

As can be expected, a wide variety of trees and flowers flourish in Havana's climate. The royal palm (Cuba's national tree) and other palm varieties are found here and there, especially in the suburbs. The *jaguey* shade tree and the thick-trunked ceiba are other exotic varieties that occasionally dominate a scene. Hundreds of species of orchids head the list of Havana's flowers.

Havana's beaches are to the east and west of the city, but children and youths regularly swim or bathe at the foot of the Malecón.

Ecological Conservation

Accompanying Havana's architectural restoration plans are programs for the restoration and regeneration of green areas. In 1959 there was a single square meter of "green" per inhabitant. This figure grew to 15 square meters per resident in 1999 and is projected to reach 20 square meters in the near future. Along with numerous neighborhood parks, four extensive green areas—the lungs of the city— have been developed since the 1959 revolution: **Parque Lenin, el Jardín Botánico Nacional, el Zoológico Nacional**, and the park surrounding Expocuba.

Havana's most exciting ecological project involves the local and international effort to save the Almendares River, which cuts the city in two between Vedado and Miramar.

"We can't speak of the green lungs of the city if we have a damaged spinal cord," explains Julio Reyes Villafruela, director of the future 700-hectare **Metropolitan Park of Havana**, embracing both sides of the river. Two community brigades and children from three nearby elementary schools do volunteer cleanup work, as part of an environmental education program. Already, 23 recreational areas have been activated within the park area, with a theater brigade entertaining children with environmental dramas. By the time this book is finished, the park's ecological restaurant may have been completed.

Also participating in the project are the embassies of Canada and the United Kingdom, plus various nongovernmental organizations, both Cuban and international. Reyes's goal is to make the project self-sustaining. The project involves reforestation and relocating industries away from the river or training them to be environmentally friendly.

Arriving in Havana, one is greeted by a sweet and mellow texture in the air. "That's your subjective sense of anticipation," remarked one skeptic. "Havana's air can be no different than the air in any other tropical city!"

Perhaps the sweetness of Havana's air is a figment of my imagination and the fantasy of so many other visitors who allow themselves to become seduced by this "agile remedy for all catastrophes."

LA HABANA

PLACES OF INTEREST
1.-Castillo del Morro (El Morro)
2.-Castillo de la Punta (La Punta)
3.-Estación Central (railroad terminal)
4.-Hotel Nacional de Cuba
5.-Coppelia ice cream palace
6.-Universidad de La Habana
7.-Terminal de Omnibus Nacionales (bus terminal)
8.-Jose Martí monument
9.-Plaza de la Revolución
10.-Estadio Latinoamericano
11.-Cementerio de Colón
12.-Teatro Karl Marx
13.-Consulatoría Jurídica Internacional
14.-Maqueta de la Ciudad
15.-Cira Garcia International Clinic

Compliments of the Cuban Embassy in Paris.

SOCIAL SETTING:
The Allure of Habaneros

Human relations between Habaneros and foreigners are affected by a bizarre social reality—the product of distorted historical scenarios and irreconcilable currencies. The purpose of this chapter is to facilitate healthy relations between foreign visitors and their Havana hosts by getting past the social barriers that emerge from this dual economy. To this end, the chapter is divided into three parts. "Here We Are" juxtaposes images of the current Havana social scenario through diverse and contradictory profiles of city residents. In "How We Got Here," we elaborate on the bizarre historical foundations of this social scenario. With the awareness gained from the first two sections, "Where We Go From Here" can now guide the visitor to truly rewarding interaction with the people of Havana. Let's get to know some Habaneros and see what this is all about.

HERE WE ARE

Tracking down Elpidio Valdez

Renato is a member of Havana's disorganized brigade of disaffected youth. Progress, he believes, can only be achieved by hustling on the streets. On a previous visit to the city, the charming Renato approached me near the Malecón and asked if I wanted to buy cigars at a bargain price.

His buoyant spirit and expressive eyes would have been assets in countries where actors and pop singers are picked up off the streets on the basis of their appearance and personality. Renato is what Cubans call a mulatto, a combination of Spaniard and African. At his side is his faithful squire and apprentice, Beto, a white Cuban flashing a perpetual smile.

Hordes of hustlers—good ones, mediocre ones, bad ones, and ones who could run a corporation—lurk in the shadowy streets in the city's hotel districts. I applied my hustler test to Renato. **Tip!** To discern between mediocre and inventive hustlers, ask for something that is impossible to find. If he says he can get it for you, you've probably got the right man.

"I don't need cigars. I need two photos," I said. "Can you find me one photo of a cane cutter and another from the city of Santiago. And I need them in black and white."

These were the two images I was missing for a book.

"Give me a day," he said, without naming his price. "Meet me right here tomorrow at this time, and maybe I'll have them."

"Five dollars per photo," I said. "That okay?"

"Fine. What's your name?" he asked.

I jotted down my name on a scrap of paper. He read my scribbles.

"Ah, Cramer. Like in *Kramer Vs. Kramer.*"

"You got it."

The next day at the same park bench, the agile Renato, not a bad basketball player when he wasn't out hustling (a shrewd point guard), showed up with the smiling Beto tagging along. The themes I'd needed were difficult enough to find, but my black-and-white requirement should have made his scavenger hunt impossible. Just in case, I came to the bench prepared to fork out ten dollars and throw in one of my T-shirts as well.

The approaching Renato flashed a prize-winning smile, holding up the photos as he swaggered over. I feared the worst: having to tell him that the photos weren't high-quality enough for my publishers. But the pictures were striking, clean-cut, and could have been taken by a professional.

Since that afternoon, Renato and I would see each other from time to time, with brief chats about the street. During the Soviet presence, he had been too young to appreciate Cuba's subsidized lifestyle; the abuses of the Batista era were distant abstractions. Renato's formative years coincided with Cuba's severe depression of the 1990s. At first he had accepted that the U.S. blockade as responsible for his privations. But the Special Period extended, eroding his optimism. He quit his job and took to the streets. He treasured the material possessions he could purchase with the privileged dollars he earned from tourists: a shiny belt, a leather wallet, a T-shirt advertising a foreign brand name. Tourism was supposed to bring prosperity to Cuba, wasn't it?

The day I was leaving Havana, the two of us shook hands, with Renato suggesting, "How about if we swap wallets?" It was an uneven trade, totally in his favor, but I gladly accepted.

A year and a half later, I returned to Havana, finding a room in the same neighborhood. With me were Renato's photos and his address. I intended to return his photos and thank him again. I was waiting for friend in a hotel lobby, studying my map of Havana. Out of the corner of my eye, a nimble figure moved by like a point guard. There was a familiar face, but my mind had been fixed on the Almendares River and all I could do was stare.

"Cramer," he shouted, "as in *Kramer Vs. Kramer!*"

"Renato!" I remembered, taking out his photos from my shirt pocket. He held up my old wallet like a banner. He was beaming. We talked for awhile.

"I've had to take a job at the Ministry of Health," he said. "With the new laws, the police are checking up on us. It got too hot for Beto, so he moved to another neighborhood and got a job."

I had spent part of my day searching for classic copies of Elpidio Valdez comic books. Elpidio Valdez was a fictional hero of Cuba's war of independence. None of the used bookstores had any, and the proprietors warned me that Elpidio was a tough find. I mentioned this to Renato.

"I'll try," he said. "But I can't say when I'll have them."

"Where do we meet?" I asked.

"I'll find you, don't worry."

The next day, I was strolling with two friends on El Prado. I heard a voice call out, "Cramer." I saw a some magazines under his arm and I knew he'd tracked down Elpidio Valdez.

I presented him to my friends, we did our business, and he disappeared into the dark, narrow streets of Centro Habana, tracking down more clients, avoiding the ubiquitous policemen who were now stationed on every corner in Havana's hotel districts.

I hope that a supervisor in the Ministry of Health will somehow discover Renato's talent and provide a ray of hope for his future. What Renato doesn't appreciate is that he's living in a historic baroque building whose apartments would rent for US$600 per month in an open market, and that he's paying a subsidized US$1.50 a month. He doesn't appreciate that he could go back to school for free and study a profession.

"Why study," I'm sure he thinks to himself, "if I'm making more than a doctor right here on the street?"

Iris and Liván

How is it that Renato, a street hustler with incomplete studies, is earning more than Iris and Liván, university graduates and professional engineers? For the answer, let's explore the background of this couple, who live in a small apartment in Vedado with their two-year-old daughter, Valentina.

Iris's mother was one of the original members of the literacy brigade. In the early '60s, she had lived for a year with an illiterate family in the Oriente in a typical, thatched-roof *bohío*. After her adopted family had learned to read and write, she was promoted to the position of schoolteacher. She identified with the revolution.

Liván's parents were of a rural background, and had witnessed the post-revolution progress in their home town of Pinar del Río, a western, tobacco-growing region of Cuba. Through his parents, Liván heard the horror stories of the Batista era.

"The ration system today is largely symbolic," Liván tells me, as he reels off a laundry list of government "errors."

"But you saw when Valentina was sick, how the clinic on our block took care of her, and how her food and clothing are provided for. We see all kinds of things that could be better, but when there's an election and we consider the alternatives, we vote for Fidel."

Liván and Iris, looking like a middle-class couple from a North American suburb, are typical believers in the Cuban process. They have no relatives in Miami and are thus excluded from the dollar economy. They watch the Renatos making more money out on the street, and they accept "such aberrations that come with tourism and the dollarization of part of Cuba's economy." Because of the U.S. trade embargo, they believe, Cuba had no choice but to obtain hard currency elsewhere. "Even back in the '80s," Liván explains, "Cuban leaders admitted that the Soviet model was an economic disaster and began enacting reforms. As

42

time goes by, some of the wrinkles in the system will be ironed out."

"There's plenty of criticism in Cuba," Iris adds. "You've seen *Fresa y Chocolate*, which condemned the previous policy toward homosexuals. A fine film it was. That's Gutiérrez Alea, our greatest director!"

"I also enjoyed his *Guantanamera*," I remark.

"It was funny," Iris says, "but Fidel didn't like it. He had to accept it because Gutiérrez Alea did so much for the revolution. But the film was unfairly critical. Cuba is under siege, and at this time, we can't afford to weaken from within."

Liván and Iris invite me to sleep over for the night. I feel guilty. Their combined incomes add up to no more than US$35 a month and they're offering me a free room.

"Only if you allow me to pay you," I say. "I'd have paid for a room somewhere else."

"How embarrassing," Iris says. "We're not renting rooms. We only want to invite you."

"At least allow me to treat you to a *paladar* dinner," I say, and they seem relieved that the rent idea has been banished from the conversation. Knowing they're not going to accept any rent, I sneak out before dinner and find a gift for their daughter. That evening, Liván is careful to pick out an inexpensive *paladar*. He is surprised when I choose a vegetarian dish.

"We Cubans think we're not eating if meat is not part of the meal," he says.

In the morning, they prepare a fine breakfast for me—eggs, black beans, milk, and rich, dark Cuban coffee. When I'm about to leave, I put Valentina's gift on the table.

"How embarrassing," Iris repeats, suspecting that I'm giving them the equivalent of rent.

"This is a custom in my country," I explain. "When we're invited to a home, we bring gifts for the children."

Pizza Stand

A few blocks from Plaza de la Revolución, I see a walled patio in front of a stucco house with a makeshift sign reading, "Pizza, $6.00." That's six pesos, or about 26 cents of a U.S. dollar. Refresco, a watery fruit punch, goes for one peso. Inside, I lean on the picnic table and chat with the proprietor as I eat my pizza.

"This is not a business, it's just a way of getting by," the woman says. She's about 60 years old, sinewy and strong. "We have to pay our taxes at the beginning of the month. If sales are low for the month, then we lose. There's no refund, no compassion."

"Why the high taxes?" I ask.

"The government doesn't want a class of people engaged in commerce to rise above the rest."

In order to conduct this business, she receives dollars from abroad. Yes, there is a commerce class emerging, I suspect: the ones who receive dollars from abroad (most of whom are white, since most Cuban exiles are white). A mere US$100 gift represents six months of a typical Cuban's salary. People like Iris and Liván, with no relatives in the United States or Spain, have no chance to compete.

I am discouraged by the complaints of the pizza seller, and I later mention my experience to a government official.

"You're right," he says. "We Cubans tend to go to one extreme or the other. In the interest of equality, we give everyone the same monthly ration. But that's not fair, because some people need more than others. We're studying a way in which we can give more rations to the ones who have no access to dollars."

Fidel's Millions?

Having lived in other Latin American countries where tax money finds its way into the pockets of corrupt politicians (and where corrupt business people avoid paying taxes), I wonder what happens with the contributions of people like the pizza seller. Iris and

Liván assure me that taxes go to sustaining the free health care system, subsidized housing, universal education, a large menu of free cultural events, and the dwindling, symbolic, food ration. But Pepe, a taxi driver who listens to Radio Martí's anti-revolution message, says the money goes into the tourist industry, where all kinds of medicines and foods, unavailable to the average Cuban, are on the shelves for tourists in "dollar stores" that only accept U.S. currency.

"That's corrupt," he says.

In various studies on the most corrupt nations in Latin America, Cuba has never earned a column inch. But *Forbes* magazine once listed Fidel Castro's personal wealth at US$1.4 billion. (The same Fidel who is so proud that Cuba has no millionaires.) Florida journalist and Cuba expert Steve Weissman set out to find out how *Forbes* had come up with the privileged information. He grilled a staff writer at *Forbes* who had worked on the team that put together an article on the world's richest kings, queens, and dictators. The reporter explained to Weissman that they had made a rough estimate. To calculate Fidel's wealth, they had taken Cuba's current gross domestic product—which then stood at US$14 billion—and decided that Fidel controlled 10 percent.

"Why not 100 percent?" asked the probing Weissman.

"We tried to be conservative," said the Forbes staffer, who admitted that they had no evidence of any stock certificates, secret bank accounts, or dividends from sugar or mineral investments, insisting that the 10 percent was "an editorial decision."

"Fidel might well have a secret stash," wrote Weissman, "but *Forbes* found nothing to prove it."

His conclusion: "*Forbes* made it up."

Credibility Problems

Fidel doesn't only have credibility problems in the United States. One afternoon, I was chatting among friends in a second-floor balcony apartment in Centro Habana. Hugo, a professor of finance at the University of Havana, was explaining to me how economists like him would tolerate their extremely low salaries if the government would at least consult with them for public policy decisions.

The topic shifted to food, and in particular, health food. I asked if anyone knew where I could get some soy yogurt. If I was ever going to live permanently in Cuba, I said, I'd need a source of soy products.

Hugo's grin was accompanied by a chorus of laughs.

"And we thought soy yogurt was no good," he said, "because Fidel recommends it."

A Believer in Soy Yogurt

It's a short flight to Santiago de Cuba in the Oriente. An alternative is the all-night train, leaving Havana's Central Station late afternoon at 4:50 p.m. and arriving in Santiago early the next morning—about a 13-hour ride. Rogelio is on the train. A former athlete, he works as a treasurer for a government sports research association. He's traveled to South America as an invited consultant, advising coaches and athletes.

Rogelio lives in an apartment in Vedado. He looks like a middle-class Vedado resident. Now in his 40s, firmly built, crew cut, unassuming, he looks fit enough for the Olympics. He knows the great boxing champion, Teófilo Stevenson. Like just about every Cuban you see, he's clean-cut and well-groomed. He believes in soy yogurt and other dietary advice that comes from Fidel and his advisors.

He smiles as he points out the landmarks of his beloved Havana, a section of the old rampart, an old stone fortress. Once we're out of the city, he looks at my map and suggests which non-tourist neighborhoods would be most interesting for my research: Regla, Cerro, Arroyo Naranjo, Guanabacoa.

It seems incongruous that he's on this train. He could have arrived in Santiago in less than two hours by hopping on a flight. I get off at Matanzas, and only after the train becomes a dot on the horizon does it dawn on me—I should have asked Rogelio, how it is that the treasurer of a government agency is using proletarian transportation? . . .

Government Crackdown

The question is, during the government crackdown against "a carnival of hissing hustlers offering women, cigars, rooms, potency medicine, and even adjustments to rental-car odometers," who is more likely to be stopped by the police: the 70-year-old Amelia, who lives according to the street economy, or a government vice-minister?

Amelia sells home-cooked lunches, illegally, in her dark, rickety, Old Havana apartment, for "whatever you wish to pay." I visit her again after not having seen her for nearly two years, and she remembers me. We embrace, and I've got to be careful not to crush her spinal cord. She's so thin she looks transparent. But she's tough and energetic.

Before the government crackdown on crime, she'd been robbed and assaulted while she was out selling peanuts. She shows me the scar on her leg. She applauds the added police presence.

We sit down for lunch. She offers me chicken or pork from her always well-stocked kitchen, but I just want rice and beans (the best rice and beans in Havana) and a salad. She has Montecristo cigars on sale for a buck. They're factory rejects, but that's only a question of looks. They're great smokes and I buy five of them. She throws in an extra cigar, on the house, and gets down to business.

"If you want to bring a girlfriend here," she says, "you can use my bedroom, or I can rent you my bedroom for the whole night, and I'll sleep down here on the sofa."

Amelia will do anything for business. Over a cup of coffee she springs another proposition.

"We could get married for business reasons," she says. "Don't worry. You wouldn't have to have sex with me."

"Amelia," I say. "During the police crackdown, how can you get away with all these businesses? Renting your room, selling lunches and cigars. They never bother you?"

"Oh, not me," she says. "Remember I once had that snack stand? I paid taxes then. They're not gonna bother me."

About the time Amelia and I were engaging in this revealing conversation, a government vice-minister was driving to the beach for a relaxing Saturday afternoon. He was wearing a T-shirt and shorts. At a traffic light, he was stopped by a policeman.

"Your ID," the cop ordered.

"I'm a vice-minister in the government," he said.

"Your ID."

Fortunately he had his carnet. The policeman scrutinized the information on the card, then stared into the eyes of the driver.

"So how can you dress like that?" he admonished, divulging his impressionist motive for having stopped the Minister.

"What else should I wear for the beach?" asked the vice-minister.

More on the Crackdown

Around midnight on a Saturday, two of my friends, Toto and his sister Soledad, have been stopped on El Prado, just for walking with me. The stern policeman won't let me intervene. Knowing Toto, he's thinking they'd been stopped because he and his sister are black. It's the percentages. More blacks are out hustling than whites, because fewer blacks have family members in Miami sending them dollars. Cuba's achievement of racial equality is under assault, and dollarization is the culprit.

"Your carnets," he said.

Toto is furious. "What right do you have? . . ."

Soledad whispers to me: "Toto doesn't know how to talk in situations like this. I'm worried."

I try again to intervene. The policeman motions me to step aside. Fumbling for his work ID, Toto explains he's a scientist working for the agriculture department. With his portable phone, the cop calls the precinct, asks for any police records on Toto and Soledad, finds none, apologizes with an *está bien*, and lets us go.

I complain about this to my government friend.

"Things were getting bad out there," he says. "The situation was threatening our whole way of life. Drugs were being sold. There were the *jineteras* [occasional prostitutes]. Two tourists were murdered. We couldn't sit by and watch the subversion from within.

"We know the newer policemen need more training. Remember, our police don't carry weapons! We're trying to create a safe environment and defend our way of life in the most humane way possible. You didn't find any of this police presence in places like Matanzas or Trinidad, did you? Not even in most neighborhoods of Havana. Just around the hotels."

"That's true," I admit.

My friend then paraphrases Fidel Castro's declaration that the battle against crime is of "enormous economic and political transcendence," comparing crime with a "fifth column" that is attacking the socialist system from within. Cuban authorities see the cleaning up of illegal activities as so vital to their society's well-being that they pay policemen more than doctors, so as to avoid corruption. They continue to ask their police to get the job done without carrying a weapon. Weaponless police are still possible in Havana, for even when things had been getting out of hand by Cuban standards, this city was much safer than Los Angeles or Washington, D.C.

But Pepe has a different opinion. Pepe, the Radio Martí-listening taxi driver, is furious about the police crackdown.

"I had one rider who came here for a two-week vacation, for the women. When he couldn't find any women out on the street, after two days, he asked me to drive him back to the airport. This is doing tremendous damage to our business."

"But Pepe," I said. "Don't you Cuban men resent the fact that foreigners were coming here to take your women?"

"That's no problem with me. Those men, they probably were tired of their wives and wanted to feel what it was like to touch smooth skin again without wrinkles. What's wrong with that?"

For Fidel, it was wrong. He had expressed outrage that Havana was becoming a haven for sex tourism.

The economics are simple. In Los Angeles, California, a prostitute earns one day's pay with one or two tricks. But given the discrepancy between Cuban and foreign currency, one informal trick by a Cuban *jinetera* is the equivalent of two or three months' salary! Couple this phenomenon with the near collapse of the Cuban economy in the wake of the loss of Soviet trade and the subsequent stiffening of the U.S. trade embargo, and anyone who does arithmetic can understand why a Cuban woman who works in an office, or even as a university professor, might be tempted to escort a foreign visitor through an evening of entertainment that might end up in a hotel bedroom. Recognizing that the phenomenon is purely economic, Olga Gasaya, vice-chair of the Department of Psychology at the University of Havana said that prior to the crackdown, "only a small percentage [of women affected by the economic crisis] resort to prostitution."

Mexican border cities across from the United States suffer from a similar inequality of currencies, with thousands of sex tourists escaping from their Puritan land to the legendary brothels just south of the border. In some Mexican border-town hotels, they won't rent you a room by the night because they make much more renting by the hour. The analogy between Mexico and Cuba is superficial, however, and is mentioned here only to illustrate how social aberrations may be rooted in bizarre economic juxta-positions, and that the world judges Cuba by stricter standards.

Clearly, visitors to Cuba who wish to establish healthy friend-ships and cultural exchange will have to deal with this totally unbalanced confrontation between two irreconcilable monetary systems. In other Latin American countries, where poverty is equivalent to misery and where the poor, for the most part, are too uneducated to have raised expectations, tourists are segre-gated from the poor by class and cultural distinctions. Cuba rep-resents an idiosyncratic exception. There is no misery here, but in its place, economic distress is generalized across suppressed class boundaries. The bottom-portion majority of Cuban society lives a significantly superior quality of life than the impoverished ma-jorities of other Latin nations, and probably better than the in-habitants of U.S. ghettos, whose quality-of-life statistics languish at the Third World level, and whose neighborhoods are infested with drugs and gangs. In Cuba, you can share a conversation about existentialism or Don Quixote with people who make US$15 a month. You become friends, and they wish they could invite you to dinner as you can so easily do for them.

I identify with this scenario in a personal way, for I have worked for extended periods of my life in countries with weak currencies, living comfortably, but within the economic param-eters of writers and artists of those countries. On trips to the United States, I suddenly became a poor person in relation to my friends. One friend would regularly insist on picking up the tab at restau-rants, thinking, "Well he comes from a country where a univer-sity professor makes six dollars an hour. No way am I going to let him pay."

Dealing with the human consequences of unbalanced econo-mies threatened to wound my pride. This is what Iris was feeling when I gave a gift for her baby. She and her husband were profes-sionals with a vague equivalent to a middle-class view of life, as was I. We had a lot in common, but a quirky monetary system was driving a wedge between us. If my gift were in any way construed as a handout, the pride of Iris and Liván would have been wounded.

The Bohemianization of Ramón

Like Iris and Liván, Ramón is a talented professional with no source of dollars. Just before the fall of the Soviet Union, he earned a scholarship to study biology at a university in Eastern Europe. He learned English, French, and German. He finished his degree at the competitive University of Havana. He has published six scientific papers. He works for a government science agency and uses his considerable computer skills, while earning US$14 month. Unlike Iris and Liván, Ramón is bitter about his predicament.

"My family supported me with great sacrifice so that I could earn a university degree, but for the past eight years [parallel to the Special Period], I've lived a disastrous economic situation. People who don't have 5 percent of my studies live a hundred times better than I do in my tiny room, sleeping on a family sofa, with virtually no personal possessions."

I later found that Ramón had also published short stories, won scholarly awards, and could analyze Plato and Kant as well as Oggún and Changó (Santerían *orishas*, or saints).

What do I do when I befriend a person like Ramón, my cultural superior thanks to a fine education system in Cuba, who cannot afford to eat in the Hanoi Restaurant for two dollars? The dilemma for the visitor is how to differentiate between a majority of Cubans, like Iris and Liván, who ask for nothing, and others who are hoping to gain something in a relationship with a foreigner. There's a trickier grey area between the extremes, a type of friend like Ramón who asks for no handout but sees me as a person who might rescue him from his dilemma.

Curiously, if Ramón, a believer in Che Guevara, should one day choose to leave Cuba, it will be because of the inequalities of capitalist reforms (why some make so much more than others) rather than the equalities of socialism. Should Ramón end up in the United States, Senator Jesse Helms will say, "I told you so; communism doesn't work," while Fidel will say, "I told you so; we should have never allowed the incursion of the dollar economy."

It gets so tricky, meeting so many good people in Havana — charming and challenging people who find themselves in such a cockeyed situation: culturally on a par with the Upper East Side of Manhattan or the Sixteenth Arrondissment of Paris, and economically on a par with a French *chômeur* or an East Harlem tenement dweller. Before confronting this human dilemma head-on, it is important to understand how we got to this social scenario, whose contradictions are especially evident in Cuba's two largest cities, Havana and Santiago.

HOW WE GOT HERE:
FOREIGN PRESENCE IN CUBAN HISTORY

The first foreigners to arrive on this island were the Spaniards (in 1512), and they quickly disposed of the native inhabitants by overworking them, giving them European diseases, or by using military violence (like the crushing of the revolt led by Taino Indian chief Hatuey in 1513). The Spanish colonials apparently had a right to do this because the Indians were pagans who did primitive things like take baths.

The Spaniards assumed the role of locals and brought in the next wave of foreigners: Africans. The global plantation and mining economies depended on slavery. The most prominent African culture was the Yoruba-speaking *lucumí* from West Africa. Slavery lasted longer in Cuba and Brazil than in other countries in the Western Hemisphere, and the resulting segregation may partially explain how African religious beliefs have endured.

During the nineteenth century, the offspring of Spaniards, referred to as criollos (or creoles), felt discriminated against by

53

The burning of Hatuey by Spanish colonials. (Picture provided by Tomás Burgos.)

the Spanish crown, and in turn the Spaniards felt that being born in the Americas was a step down from being born in Spain. Something about the air in the Americas that made you inferior.

Independence Wars

Most Latin American countries earned their independence in the 1820s. Decades later, Cuba was still a colony when in 1868, creole landowner Carlos Manuel de Céspedes launched an independence revolt. After Céspedes was ambushed and shot down by the Spaniards, a Cuban mulatto named Antonio Maceo continued the insurgency.

José Martí

From this time on, Cuban rebels welcomed foreign revolutionaries. The original Che of Cuban history was Máximo Gómez, an immigrant from Santo Domingo. The insurgency failed, but in

54

1895, Gómez and Maceo were joined by poet and lawyer José Martí, the founder of the Partido Revolucionario Cubano, who since 1869 had been publishing editorials and other literature in favor of Cuban independence. His philosophy went beyond calls for political independence and preached social equality and the abolition of racism. Due to his political activities, Martí was exiled from Cuba twice, in 1871 and 1879.

Martí did not want the economy of Cuba geared to the needs of a foreign market—a situation that was the essence of colonialism. Little did he know (he died in battle in 1895) that following Cuba's belated and nominal independence in 1902, the island would pass through a lengthy period as a supplier of raw materials for the United States, which owned most of the mines and the sugar plantations that were Cuba's only real industries. Most Cubans believe that Martí's independence struggle did not truly end until the triumph of the 1959 Revolution. But subsequent support from the Soviet Union, generous as it was, made it expedient for Cuba to maintain its monocultural sugar production, an economic model that Cuban authorities regarded as unacceptable by the 1980s, when they began to initiate reforms that included mixed private and public enterprises. Typically, colonized countries export raw materials to industrialized countries, then buy back their own raw materials in the form of more expensive finished products.

The writings of Martí clearly define a stance against economic, political, and military domination by the United States. The last letter he wrote before he died illustrates the reason he was fighting so desperately against the Spanish occupation. Cuba needed to defend herself "through independence, before it's too late, to stop the United States from encroaching into the Antilles and pouncing with force upon our lands."

We wanted to ask Martí his opinions about the Miami radio station, Radio Martí, which in his name supports the U.S. economic embargo against Cuba and exhorts Cubans to yield to the United States by overthrowing their government. He was unavailable for comment.

Independence?

After the Cuban nationalists had softened up the Spaniards and victory was inevitable, the United States moved in. The pretext was the 1898 explosion of the USS *Maine*, a battleship which was anchored in the Havana harbor to protect U.S. investments; 260 crew members were killed. Cubans allege that the *Maine* was blown up on purpose to fabricate grounds for an invasion. The resulting Spanish-American War ensued for four months. After the United States finished off the Spaniards, the Cubans weren't even invited to the 1898 peace treaty ceremony in Paris. The new occupiers, seeing that victorious Cuban rebel leader Calixto García and most of his troops were black, decided to temporarily leave municipal governments in the hands of the Spaniards.

Instead of independence, Cuba gained U.S. military occupation that lasted until 1902. Although nominal independence was eventually granted to the Cubans, the 1901 Platt Amendment thwarted Cuban self-determination, allowing for military intervention whenever U.S. business interests were threatened. The Platt Amendment also allowed for the establishment of a U.S. naval base at Guantánamo in 1903. Today the base (off-limits to Cubans) is the only place in Cuba where you can get a McDonald's Big Mac.

The Batista Years

Cuba's republican years were marked by political turmoil. In 1934, instigated by U.S. ambassador Sumner Wells, Cuban sergeant Fulgencio Batista staged a military coup. The Treaty of Reciprocity of 1935 gave preferential treatment to U.S. exports in Cuba, and Batista kept labor costs down for U.S. employers by crushing a labor rebellion the same year. Batista, supported by the Cuban Communist Party (which later denied support to the Castro revolution), won rigged elections in 1940.

Cuba became a playground for affluent North American tourists and a haven for Mafia-related activities. The statistics said Cuba's economy was doing well, but this was a two-tiered economy: one level for the wealthy minority (mainly criollos) and another for the poor and illiterate majority (many of whom were black). Batista had an image problem abroad, and even at home, his countrymen refused to let him join the Havana Yacht and Country Club because he was mulatto.

Fidel

With Batista looking like a bad guy, the Cuban Revolution had plenty of support from abroad, and Fidel Castro would eventually be portrayed as a good guy in the *New York Times*. It must be understood that revolutionary ferment existed in Cuba years before Fidel Castro rose to prominence.

Castro's first move was a bold attack on the Moncada army barracks on July 26, 1953. Of his 119 insurgents, 55 were massacred. The young lawyer Castro was captured and tried. His defense statement became the famous document, "History Will Absolve Me." He was sentenced to 15 years.

He got lucky when Batista, under enormous pressure from the Cuban population and progressive countries abroad, liberated all political prisoners. In exile in Mexico with his brother Raúl, Castro met Ernesto "Che" Guevara, an Argentine doctor, adventurer, and asthmatic. In 1956, this revolutionary trio returned to Cuba on the yacht *Granma* and began their military campaign from the Sierra Maestra mountains in the Oriente. Che's outnumbered troops won a decisive victory against the Batista army at Santa Clara on December 17, 1958. Batista then fled Havana on January 1, 1959, emptying the Cuban national treasury. Che and guerrilla leader Camilo Cienfuegos entered Havana victoriously on January 2, with Fidel Castro joining them six days later.

(Che Guevara would eventually depart for more revolutionary adventures in Africa and Bolivia. In Bolivia, his guerrilla campaign failed and he was executed. Che's legacy in Cuba is his conception of the "New Man," who is motivated to work for humanistic rather than material reasons—this was his ambitious, unfinished project. Today, El Che is still revered by many Cubans of all ideological stripes.)

So who pushed first? Could Fidel have been a communist from the outset, even though his nationalist revolution had been spurned by the Cuban Communist Party? Was the Cuban Revolution pushed into the arms of the Soviets when Fidel was snubbed by President Dwight Eisenhower and made the target of CIA assassination attempts, including the infamous exploding cigars that failed to explode? Or did the United States decide to clamp down on Cuba when U.S.-owned properties and businesses, like the United Fruit Company, were expropriated in the name of desperately needed agrarian reform?

When the U.S. suspended Cuba's sugar quota in 1960, was Cuba obligated to seek a new Sugar Daddy in the Soviet Union? President Eisenhower presented the suspension of the sugar quota as a retaliation for the expropriations, but the U.S. ambassador to Cuba at the time, Philip Bonsal, has remarked that "the suspension of the sugar quota was a major element in the program to overthrow Castro." This program, according to historian Tad Szulc, was part of an "already constituted top-secret policy in March of 1959."

The year 1961 saw the ill-fated, CIA-backed Bay of Pigs invasion. Could this have been the final straw that hardened Fidel into an ideologue, or was Castro always a strict paternalist who, even without harassment from the United States, would have become an authoritarian leader?

Escalations

The antagonism between the United States and Cuba nearly exploded in 1962 with the Cuban missile crisis, which was eventually resolved when the Soviets, without consulting the Cubans, agreed to withdraw their missiles from Cuban soil. Under pressure from the Cuban government, the U.S. pledged to not invade Cuba as part of a complex agreement.

By the 1970s, President Richard Nixon was opening commercial channels with the United States' most feared rivals, the Soviet Union and China. Yet the trade embargo against tiny Cuba endured throughout the 1990s, even after the far-more repressive Chinese regime was receiving "most-favored-nation" trading status. Cuban political leaders must have felt flattered that this tiny island of only 11 million inhabitants was perceived as a threat to the United States.

Meanwhile, the Cuban Revolution had amassed a number of unprecedented achievements. The extensive illiteracy from the Batista times was eradicated in 1961 through a campaign which saw middle-class, urban students volunteer to live in primitive conditions with illiterate rural families, teaching family members of all ages to read and write. Many of Cuba's doctors had left the country after the triumph of the Revolution. A whole new crop of idealistic physicians was trained, and within a decade, the country had one of the world's most successful universal health care systems. Private schools were outlawed and a successful public education system created equal rights for all. With racism forcibly abolished, most of Cuba's professions were thoroughly integrated. Both culture and sports were made accessible to every Cuban citizen, and Cuba became Latin America's leader in quality cinema and Olympic gold medals.

The consciousness industry had most of us believing that Cuba was an uncritical partner of the Soviet Union. Yet Cuba defied the Soviets by becoming a leader of the nonaligned na-

Literacy brigadier Rosita (at right) with the rural community she taught to read and write. In the background is her thatch-roofed bohío.

tions. Meanwhile, Russians living in Cuba suffered from perpetual culture shock and often remained in monocultural enclaves. At the same time, cultural affinities between Cuba and the United States could not be suppressed. Many Cubans successfully learned English, and Cuba, to its own detriment, retained a technological infrastructure — symbolized by the 110 volt electric system — that required unobtainable spare parts from the United States, when they could have shifted to European or Japanese technologies. Such affinities with the United States ironically increased the effectiveness of the economic embargo.

Serious errors were made in the agricultural arena. Soviet subsidies were contingent on the Russians receiving an ample supply of sugar. Out of expedience, the country retained its monocultural agriculture based on sugar cane instead of diversifying. By the 1980s, Cuban leaders had begun to reform this system, but their dependency on food imports and pesticides from Eastern Europe left Cuba in a most vulnerable situation when the Soviet Union collapsed in 1990.

Suddenly, with insufficient food production to feed its population, Cuba was obligated to transform its whole agricultural system to an organic model. Meanwhile, the United States was expanding the embargo with new, more restrictive legislation. Appalling food, medicine and fuel shortages led to the infamous "Special Period in a time of peace."

The U.S. Economic Embargo

The degree to which the nearly four-decade economic embargo impacts Cubans' quality of life is debatable. Cuban authorities insist the embargo should be called a "blockade." Foreign diplomats stationed in Havana told this writer off the record that the reality was somewhere in between.

Whatever you call it, certain facts speak for themselves. The embargo, whose stated rationale was to stop Soviet influence in Cuba, was nevertheless stiffened after the departure of the Soviets. The 1992 Torriceli Act prohibits foreign subsidiaries of U.S. corporations from trading with Cuba and places a six-month ban on ships that have docked in Cuban ports. The 1996 Helms-Burton Act allows U.S. investors to take action in U.S. courts against foreign companies that utilize property confiscated in Cuba after the Revolution. This means that certain medicines and parts of medical machinery that are exclusively manufactured by non-U.S. companies with ties to U.S. pharmaceutical corporations cannot be purchased by Cuba. It also means that a significant tourist market from the United States is coerced into not visiting Cuba. And it means that when Cuba purchases items from Europe or Asia that could have been purchased from the United States, Cuban companies must spend millions of dollars per year in debilitating shipping costs. This is wasted money that could have been used to maintain the country's universal health care and education system, increase the monthly food ration, or repair deteriorating infrastructure.

The nonpartisan American Association for World Health (AAWH), stationed in Washington, D.C. and chaired by Dr. Peter G. Bourne (a former cabinet member of the Jimmy Carter administration) believes that "the inclusion of food and medicine in an international trade embargo is a violation of international human rights conventions which uphold the principle of a free flow of food and medicines, even in wartime, to serve the basic needs of civilian populations." Both the AAWH and another nonpartisan humanitarian organization, OXFAM-International, publish reports documenting the suffering of Cuban citizens, in terms of health and nutrition, which results directly from the U.S. embargo. But the AAWH also adds that "Cuba's health statistics more closely approximated those of the nations of Europe and North America than of developing countries," and that "the infant mortality rate in Cuba is roughly half that of Washington, D.C."

If the intention of the embargo was to weaken Fidel, say some critics, then the embargo is a total failure, for many Cubans who might have opposed their top leader instead rallied behind him in the face of a foreign threat. Richard Nixon, an important influence in the approval of a 1960 covert action program against Castro, reflected in 1994 that "the hard line has failed," and that "the administration should drop the economic embargo and open the way to trade, investment, and economic interaction."

Year after year, the United States is totally outnumbered in the U.N. General Assembly in votes on the embargo. Even Israel, one of only two countries to vote along with the U.S. in 1997 in support of the embargo, has opened trade relations with Cuba.

Double Vision
When I first traveled to Cuba, I was advised that people would be afraid to talk with me about serious issues. Bad advice is so easy to find. Most people in Havana exuberantly offer their varied and contradictory opinions about Cuba's controversial social history to foreign visitors, who will be dizzied into schizophrenia by a confusing set of contrary logics.

Freedom of the Press
Freedom-of-information advocates would be turned off by the unwavering rhetoric of *Granma* (the party newspaper) and *Bohemia* (the party magazine) during the Soviet years, and the flow of information has not opened up a whole lot since. In 1997, on a scale of 1 to 10, Cuba ranked 0.9, the lowest of all Latin American countries, in the categories of access to information and free, pluralistic freedom of expression, according to the Ibero-American Forum on Communications.

Cuban spokespeople cite the economic and terrorist war against their country as the reason for controlling the press, claiming that historically, states have always controlled the flow of information when their sovereignty was in danger. They'll dazzle you with a long list of examples of threats to the Cuban state: the CIA-backed Bay of Pigs invasion of 1961; the 1976 terrorist bombing of a Cubana de Aviación flight that killed 73 people and was

63

instigated by a Cuban exile and former CIA employee; the rash of bombings of hotels and restaurants in 1997 allegedly financed by Miami-based Cuban exiles; the U.S. government's courtship with exile groups that advocate terrorism; numerous documented attempts by U.S. agents to assassinate Fidel Castro; the incessant radio messages beamed in from the United States by exiles who ask Cuban people to disrupt their system; and a four-decade "blockade." Their tiny country is under siege, they reason, by the world's dominant imperial power, and they must take whatever measures necessary to protect themselves in an uneven battle.

But a freer flow of diverse opinions would hardly make an impact on Cuba's evolving system, since these opinions gush forth orally in public and private forums anyway. When a well-meaning father doesn't allow for free and open criticism within the family, he is more likely to lose the allegiance of his children. The greatest achievement of the U.S. embargo is to have catalyzed a reaction verging on paranoia among some of Cuba's leaders.

I know of one overcautious Cuban journalist who, just to play it safe, prevented the publication of material that would have benefited his country. Ironically, the Cuban government's fine education system has improved the flow of information in a very unexpected way; I am aware of one banned book that ended up with a wide readership. In other Latin American countries with poorer education records, even the most autocratic president has no need to control the written word, since a bestseller doesn't sell more than 3,000 copies. Even banned books do better business in Cuba than bestsellers in Guatemala or Bolivia.

Human Rights

Following the Revolution, some 500 Batista supporters were executed, with a "them or us" rationale voiced by Che Guevara. Since then, Amnesty International reports show that Cuba has maintained hundreds of "prisoners of conscience," and that allowing such critics to leave the country is a convenient way of ridding the system of opposition. But contrary to virtually every other Latin American country, no Cuban military official has ever gunned down an innocent civilian, and Cuban police carry no weapons. The death squads so typical (in various periods) of Colombia, Brazil, El Salvador, Guatemala, Honduras, Mexico, Argentina, and Chile have never existed in Cuba.

"Where can you find a single victim of torture, assassination, or disappearance [in Cuba]," writes Cuban vice-president Carlos Lage, who affirms that, "for us, human rights go beyond the fundamentals listed in the Universal Declaration and include social justice, true equality, and a just distribution of wealth." Citing the existence of Puerto Rican political prisoners in the United States, Lage feels that Cuba is being unfairly singled out.

In 1987 the United Nations agreed with Lage. The U.S. had sponsored a resolution harshly criticizing Cuba for human rights violations. The resolution was voted down by the U.N. Human Rights Commission and only one of eight Latin American representatives on the commission voted with the United States.

No abuse of human rights can be tolerated or rationalized, whether it occurs in Cuba or any other country. Cuba's admirable record in enriching the lives of its least fortunate is no apology for any abuses that have been documented by Amnesty International.

Emigration

Anyone who follows the history of refugees cannot remain unmoved by the *balseros*, who, during the early 1990s, fled Cuba on makeshift rafts, hoping to make it to Florida. Similarly, the *marielitos* of 1980, some of whom today languish in U.S. prisons, defied the paradigm of previous, affluent Cuban refugees who didn't want to share their wealth and power. Fidel's having unloaded convicts and mentally ill people among the *marielitos* was crafty to say the least, and not in keeping with the most humane of his social policies.

65

In Matanzas, I had a long conversation with one former *balsero* who was picked up at sea, taken to the Guantánamo Naval Base, and then returned to Cuba after it was deemed that he had not been the victim of any political repression and was simply an economic refugee. He insists that he is now a marked man because of his *balsero* history.

One is also moved by the stories of original emigrants — those who hopped on a flight and left all their belongings and property behind, fearing that the Revolution would destroy their way of life. The scorn that they had to deal with often left permanent scars.

I have also spoken with formerly affluent Cubans — like Havana resident Lourdes, who did have the opportunity to leave but chose to stay — and have no regrets about their decision, even though they now live without wealth. Lourdes remains a dedicated supporter of the Revolution. She believes that her friends and family members who left did what they had to and understands that there were two conflicting logics in the aftermath of the Revolution.

In order to evaluate Cuban emigration, historians must decipher whether the decision to leave was political or simply economic. Furthermore, one must compare Cuban emigration with the flight of Mexicans to the United States. Is there a difference between the Cuban *balseros* and the desperate Mexican and Central American immigrants to the United States, many of whom die during their penurious odyssey or make it safely to California, Texas or Chicago, only to be scorned as "illegal aliens." Why did Mexican refugees, who fled a country ruled by a single party dictatorship, receive none of the social benefits that were heaped upon Cuban refugees? Had Mexicans been welcomed in the U.S. like the Cubans, how many Mexicans would be left in Mexico? Statistically, a greater portion of Salvadorans and Bolivians, for example, have fled their respective countries than Cubans have fled theirs.

After voting to damage the health and nutrition of Cuban citizens, U.S. congressmen may lack the moral authority to say "I told you so," when a Cuban raft arrives on the shores of Florida. Those who morally condemn Cuba's socialist system on the basis of the fact that so many people have desired to leave the country would have ample statistical and moral grounds for condemning Mexico's capitalist system for the same reason. None of this diminishes the sorrow I feel for the *balsero* in Matanzas.

Social Equality

It used to be that no Cuban earned more than four times as much as any other Cuban. With the 1990s escalation of tourism and a dollar economy, some people are becoming more "equal" than others. Benefitting most are the Cubans working in the tourist industry who receive tips in dollars and those receiving dollars from abroad. Cuban officials are committed to doing something to recover whatever social, racial, and gender equality that withered away, but they seem to be groping for a way to do it.

67

Still, one is much more likely to see groups of whites and blacks hanging out in harmony in Cuba compared to places like Chicago or Washington, D.C. But one University of Havana professor told this writer that he was frightened by the diminishing numbers of Afro-Cuban students.

The equal status of Cuban women was under siege during the Special Period, but equal pay for equal work between the sexes is still enforced, and women are equally represented in the professions. Cuba's population growth statistics are as low as in any advanced industrialized country. With fewer children per household than in most Latin American countries, Cuban women remain freer to develop their professions.

Prostitution, once nearly eliminated by revolutionary education and self-esteem measures, is back again. People who never condemned prostitution in Holland, Mexico, or Thailand are evidently holding Cuba to a higher standard. The return of prostitution is linked to the depression of the Special Period and the escalation of tourism in the early and mid-1990s. As economic indicators rise, prostitution should decline, especially since the government has finally decided to address the issue. By mid-1999, the number of *jineteras* hanging around tourist hotels had diminished, although this may be more related to repressive measures than to an increase in economic opportunities for women.

Cuba's high-quality and free-education system has produced unexpected dilemmas. Low wages are partially compensated for by heavily subsidized housing, transportation, and culture, but universal education has led to higher expectations and therefore more frustration. Potential frustrations resulting from an excess of doctors, teachers, scientists, and technicians have been partially defused by official programs in which Cuba exports medical, cultural, and technical assistance to developing countries.

There is little gap between the bottom of Cuban society and what can be loosely referred to as a middle class. Intense experiences in the shantytowns of La Paz, Mexico City, and San Salvador lead me to conclude that the bottom of Cuban society enjoys a higher quality of life than the impoverished majorities in the rest of Latin America. Professor Jon Torgerson of Drake University, an annual visitor to Cuba, insists that the bottom end of Cuban society enjoys a superior quality of life than the bottom end of American society. After having made such an outrageous statement, he was threatened with losing a grant by none other than Clarence Thomas.

But I can also testify that Cuba's well-educated and extensive middle sector lives with many more limitations than the small but privileged middle classes in the rest of Latin America. After all, a crafty Havana street hustler can easily pocket more dollars than a pediatrician.

Statistically, Cuba as a whole scores better than any other Latin American country when combining key social indicators, but this is hardly consolation for many Cuban professionals with limited buying power and little room to display their talents. One of the consolations for this class of people was the knowledge that even high-ranking Cuban officials were suffering in the same boat and did not resort to corruption as a means to get ahead of the rest. The wives of government ministers could be observed waiting in line at the bakery like any other Cuban.

But the parallel dollar economy opens the doors to greater opportunities for corrupt practices, and the simple fact that a separate and more privileged economy exists within the tourist sector is viewed by some Cubans as inherently corrupt. I know one committed communist who left the country because of such emerging inequalities.

Habanero attitudes about the nearby Varadero tourist resort, off-limits to most Cubans, reflect this duality of opinion towards the tourist industry.

"Varadero is not Cuba," said architect Miguel Coyula.

This brief and conceptual history of Cuba has been spare on dates, names and other encyclopedic appendages, as its sole purpose is to introduce readers to the social scenario they will be entering. (Refer to the bibliography for more extensive sources for Cuban history.)

I have met very few Cubans who stand unequivocally for or against their system. The two extreme points of view on Cuba, the ones that are plastered in the media, are hardly prominent on the streets and in the living rooms of Havana. Instead, a rich texture of varying opinions defies all paradigms. Some of the same people who won't eat soy yogurt because Fidel recommends it believe their country needs another Che.

WHERE WE GO FROM HERE

After having been asked to endure nearly a decade of sacrifice during the Special Period, even those Habaneros who believe that the U.S. blockade was largely responsible for their privations may yield to temptation and seek a beneficial friendship with dollar-laden tourists. Even among economic equals, it is universal for opportunism to creep into a friendship, as is evident in any text on "networking." Given these particular and universal influences on human relations, it is surprising that the majority of Habaneros ask and expect nothing from their foreign friends.

Visitors, especially those from more reserved cultures, should understand that people from Havana are outgoing and remarkably frank, and sometimes flippantly gregarious. Havana's historical sense of community, along with the Revolution's institutionalization of neighborhood-based social, medical, and political functions, makes it difficult to lead a private life. When there is a choice between public good and private rights, the public good usually wins. What some Westerner would consider "invasion of privacy" has kept guns out of the hands of citizens, suppressed street crime, and clamped down on the spread of AIDS.

Foreigners from macho cultures, where women are expected or required to be reserved, may be taken aback by the fact that in male-female relationships, women are just as likely to take the initiative as men. In an international women's flirting contest (prostitutes excluded), Cuban women would make the finals. Massive publicity for gender equality by revolutionary leaders, with the help of film makers, journalists, and school teachers has done little to dent the machismo of many Cuban men, but it has increased the spirit of independence among women. Effective sexual education and legal abortion (during the first three months of pregnancy) have given Cuba a birth rate as low as the most advanced industrialized countries. Intervention by the State in assuring basic necessities for children has liberated women from the economic bondage of marriage, so you don't find too many Cuban women who stay in a bad marriage for fear of confronting the world on their own. A typical theme in several Cuban movie classics is the conflict between a woman who demands her professional and personal independence with her man who attempts to exert the control of machismo.

These are some of the variables in today's social setting that are the product of complex cultural foundations, post-1959 revolutionary policies, the tribulations of the Special Period, the addition of capitalist nuances to the socialist economy, a stinging economic embargo, and a rapid escalation of tourism.

Given the enormous gap between the income of foreign visitors and local Habaneros, newcomers to Havana should be aware of strategies for transcending the potential for conscious or subconscious opportunism in human relationships.

Joint Projects

On the Malecón, a photographer tourist from Nebraska, who had visited Cuba seven times, told me he had forged a joint venture with a Cuban artist friend, in which they made post cards and

71

shared the profits. Their relationship became collegial and they worked as equals.

When help is mutual rather than one-sided, no one feels like a charity case and the shame factor is eliminated. The idea of joint projects of mutual interest is infinite and can be related to virtually every livelihood or common interest.

Sharing

More feasible than joint projects is the method practiced by the Vidals, owners of a photography store in Spain. They make regular trips to Havana to visit their friends, always bringing a stash of gifts. Paternalism is not a motive, only a friendship between people who are equals in every way other than their purely mathematical difference in currencies. Their Havana friends understand that this is simply a question of sharing.

Many Cuban professionals have accepted a system in which they've forfeited the rights to privilege that in other countries are linked with a professional degree. In essence, Cuban professionals are automatically doing the same thing as the Vidals, giving up material advantages so that other Cubans may enjoy an organic equality. The concept of giving as a social equalizer is intrinsic to the system.

In the socio-historical context of Havana neighbors and their CDR (Committee for the Defense of the Revolution) helping the less fortunate on their blocks, it no longer seems aberrant for a foreigner to enter a relationship of solidarity with a Cuban companion.

Seeking Wisdom

Another approach to interacting in Havana is to seek out knowledge and wisdom from the people. What interior strength or collective solidarity allowed the Cubans to survive the frightening scarcity of the early- and mid-1990s, and remain buoyant and impeccably groomed? Go explain how in the midst of pain and tribulation, the streets of Havana were alive with joyous conversation and contagious salsa music.

Serge, a former student of mine and talented keyboard musician, goes to Havana to take courses and jam with great Cuban musicians. In particular, Serge was captivated by the noncommercial and varied rhythms and textures of the music. Each Cuban group forges a distinct style, a scenario made possible, ironically, by Cuba's forced marginalization from the homogeneous, globalized top-forty music business. The trade embargo may have nurtured Cuba's musical independence.

Cubans who have lived through such an extraordinary and quirky history have much cultural wisdom to offer. That they continue to express great esteem for their counterparts in the United States shows that historical abuses do not taint personal relations. Whatever economic imbalance exists between visitors and locals can be nullified when the visitors are there to learn from Cuban culture.

In a less tangible way, I've known people from cultures that emphasize privacy who have gone to Havana, lived in a neighborhood, and learned to appreciate a more public and communal existence. It was hard for them at first, but they adjusted and then thrived. It's virtually impossible to live a private existence in many of Havana's neighborhoods, but on the other hand, Habaneros will respect your idiosyncrasies and never judge you by standards of elitism or Puritanism. A sense of community does not obliterate respect for individuality.

Foreign student Rosa Elena felt a type of "freedom" she had never before experienced in her native Bolivia or in her visits to Argentina. She summed it up as "a freedom from social pretensions." In Havana, where she lived for eight years, she felt she was able to relate to other human beings without the repressive, class-based social mores of her native country that force people to play social roles in order to maintain appearances. What would be status symbols in the United States, like a 1953 Ford or a 1961 Edsel, remain a humble part of Havana's daily funk.

In Havana, the harmless subculture of Cubans who are out to get something from tourists may deceptively appear like a major portion of the country to the hotel-confined visitor. But stroll through animated streets to another neighborhood, Regla or Arroyo Naranjo, for example, and that subculture is virtually absent, as it is in any city where tourism is not implanted. In Cárdenas, a worthy side trip from Havana, only 9 miles (15 km) from Varadero, I waited and waited to get hustled or for someone to ask me for something, but it simply didn't happen.

Even in Havana neighborhoods where tourism reaches a saturation level, once you are known to the neighbors and become involved in the daily life, you will be treated like anyone else, and will increasingly meet Cubans who want nothing from you but the sharing of ideas and eventual friendship. The mere act of changing dollars to Cuban pesos and frequenting peso establishments is a good start.

With all the bizarre contradictions of incompatible economies, healthy human relationships between foreigner visitors and Habaneros will survive and thrive once the visitor is aware of the country's social history as it is reflected in contemporary life. Even during the period when Habaneros walking with tourists were being stopped by police for an ID check, it was still easier to interact with people in this city than in any other capital city in the world.

CHAPTER THREE

GETTING AROUND:
Camels, Rail Hostesses, and the Lord of the Crossroads

Prior to my first trip to Havana, I was told by a travel agent specializing in Cuba that public transportation was irregular and that I would need to use taxis. Buses, she said, were mainly for Cuban workers, and were uncomfortable and undependable.

I didn't believe her. I understand that it's tough to get around in spread-out cities like Los Angeles, California, which are designed for and dominated by the private motor vehicle. But few Cubans own their own cars. Habaneros must have ways to get to and from work and play. And when the local Industriales baseball team plays at home, few of the fans who fill their stadium, the Estadio Latinoamericano, reside in the immediate neighborhood of Cerro. Residents manage to get to music festivals in other neighborhoods and the beaches outside of the city, and they aren't taking taxis.

The travel agent accurately noted that buses often run irregularly, and when they do arrive, they are usually crammed with straphangers. But I quickly found relatively practical ways to use these buses, some of which, including the two-humped *camellos* hauled by a truck cabin, add a bizarre component to the landscape of the city.

I later found alternatives to the buses. To get across the bay to historical communities like Regla, ferries run as regularly as the Staten Island Ferry in New York. And after a long wait, just when you've finally given up on a ride and are considering nearby lodging for the night, collective "taxis" for five passengers seem to show up. For 10 pesos (US$0.50) they get you out of a dilemma. But the cost is steep for the average Cuban accustomed to paying 40 cents of a peso (US$0.02) for a bus.

Other alternatives are walking and cycling, both of which are remarkably effective ways to get around. Strategically located Habaneros find commerce and entertainment within walking distance. Aside from a few major thoroughfares, where automobile traffic only begins to approach the volume of other major cities in the world, bicycle traffic is the primary nemesis for the pedestrian. If you can't beat this kind of traffic, you can join it.

For traveling outside the city on weekend excursions, the bus terminal near Plaza de la Revolución is relatively efficient, and the Estación Central (the Central Railroad Station) offers attractive alternatives.

It has already been emphasized that life in Havana revolves around the neighborhood, and the thrills of the city can be most appreciated by hanging out in the community and getting to know your neighbors. I know several locals who rarely leave their own neighborhood and manage to live an exciting life.

WALKING

For those who enjoy regular visits to different quarters of the city, a strategic choice of residence can drastically reduce the need for public transportation, by putting you within walking distance of Havana's greatest neighborhoods. Finding an apartment or home stay in Centro Habana, anywhere between Chinatown and Parque de la Fraternidad will place you in a central core within walking distance of Old Havana, the Malecón, Vedado, the bus station near Plaza de la Revolución, the Estación Central train station, and the Estadio Latinoamericano in Cerro. **Tip!** From this location, you'll rarely have to use any public transportation within the city, and you'll be near both bus and train stations for excursions outside the city.

With a few exceptions, Havana's streets qualify for the designation "pedestrian friendly." Motor vehicle traffic, except for avenues like the treacherous boulevard along the Malecón, is not a menace to pedestrians.

In modern urban settings, there are three types of streets: (A) empty; (B) full of indifferent people; (C) full of friendly people. Type-A streets are typically found in North American suburbs, where people use private automobiles and rarely do their daily errands on foot. Whether these people are friendly or not is hard to determine, since the chance of meeting them while strolling is dim.

Type-B streets are typified by the central cores of modern western cities, especially those cities without mixed-use zoning, where people do not live near where they do commerce. Outside the urban cores, single-use zoning and other utilitarian measures have led to a lack of public gathering places. The people in such places may be friendly but there is no place on the street to stop and express an interest in fellow human beings.

Most of Havana qualifies as a Type-C city. Neighborhoods are either of mixed use, or near enough to local commerce for

77

people to do their daily business on foot. The Havana neighbor-hood is the defining unit of the city, and is the place where people express themselves, socially and politically. Cuban neighbors know each other personally, and a new foreign neighbor will find it dif-ficult to remain anonymous within such a context.

Spontaneous events may break out on neighborhood streets—stickball or punchball games, rumba music, or simply people gathering to chat. Public gathering places such as cafes, parks, the Malecón, and the Prado (with its built-in strolling lane and benches), are ubiquitous to the city.

The street is Havana's greatest attraction. It is vibrant and full of excitement, enhanced by the city's colonial architectural treasures, tropical warmth, and the bustling informal economy. Every time you step out of your door and venture onto Havana's streets, adventure is beckoning.

BICYCLES

Cyclists have more options as to their choice of neighborhood. The most effective transportation measure for the newcomer is to pack a bicycle before leaving for Havana. Should you have any trouble putting it back together, bicycle and tire repair shops are found all over the city, as cycling is a major form of transportation for Havana residents. In the throes of the 1990s fuel crisis, Fidel Castro kicked off an ambitious cycling campaign, looking toward Holland's bicycle culture as an example of fitness and environmental friendliness. The streets in both Amsterdam and Havana are flat, but Havana's steamy summer weather is not as conducive to regular pedaling as Amsterdam's more benign summer.

An alternative to taking your own bike to Havana would be to spread the word in your adopted neighborhood that you'd like to purchase a used bike — one of the heavier, Chinese bicycles that were distributed throughout the country during the 1990s. Or, bite the bullet and purchase a new one in any of the city's major department stores. (See shopping tips in Chapter 6.) Bicycles can also be rented from major hotels for day trips.

Havana is a flat city, so a ten-speed is not necessary. A basic three-speed bike works fine, and even a single speed, if adjusted to your pedaling strength, will be functional. The negative of exclusive bicycle-dependence is the broiling summer season (May to October), which really heats up from July through September. But being squeezed into a *camello* in the summer heat may be more threatening than sweating it out in the open air on your bike.

Many Cubans do not lock their bikes after riding, since bicycle guards watch over them at designated parking areas.

CITY BUSES

Cyclists can cross the bay tunnel to beach country by taking the *cyclobus*, which has special ramps for bicycles. You can get this bus at the traffic circle by the park just before the tunnel at the end of Agramontes (also called Zulueta), just west of El Prado. Cyclists can also cross the bay to Regla via ferry at the Aduanas, or "Customs," building pier in Old Havana at the end of Santa Clara Street.

Buses cost 40 Cuban cents. The *camellos*, which reach the suburbs, cost only 20 Cuban cents (a US penny). This is quite a difference from paying five dollars for an independent taxi. Cuban buses usually pass by with overflowing cargos of passengers. But there's much more municipal control of the passenger situation than in other Latin American countries, where passengers in tilting buses are often seen hanging out the door.

A change collector within many buses organizes the passengers, and if you follow his or her advice and move to the rear, you have a fair chance of getting a seat somewhere along the way, since people who got on before you were directed to the back of the bus.

Passengers load up for a "camel" ride.

The etiquette for mounting a bus is unique to Havana. When you get to the bus stop, you ask "who was the last person" (¿Quién fue la última persona?), or simply, (¿la última?), and you follow that person onto the bus. No need to wait on a line. Waiting for buses may turn into quality chatting time. I once missed my place when I was distracted by a conversation with an old friend who was strolling by. The employee controlling the passenger traffic from within the bus was only allowing four people to board at that particular stop, since he knew more people would be boarding at subsequent stops. I explained to him that I'd missed my place, to no avail. But then the people who had boarded ahead of me told him, "He's a foreigner, let him on." It worked.

I usually find interesting conversation on Havana buses. Bus riding is not an unpleasant experience, unless one is carrying packages that can't be collapsed to fit within the crowd. People with a rushed lifestyle may have to seek other forms of transportation, as non-rush hour waiting time may be considerable.

Tip! The best way to get a seat is to catch a bus at its first stop. In some cases it may be preferable to walk to Parque de la Fraternidad in Centro Habana, where many of the main lines have their first stop. The M2 *camello* will get you to the vicinity of the airport, and the M1 carries its load between Alamar and Vedado.

In the genre of Cuban primitive art, the quirky *camello* is often the star of the painting. It always looks better in art than in real life, and one wonders how these dromedarian painters become so enamored with the *camello*.

FERRY

From the Aduanas pier at the end of Santa Clara, you can take ferries across the harbor to the interesting communities of Regla and Casablanca. There are no seats on these ferries, as room is set aside for bicycles. The service is regular, fast, and efficient. The cost: one peso. Not as cheap as the free Staten Island Ferry, and

Ferry dock in Regla.

instead of viewing the Statue of Liberty, you see a busy harbor with an industrial backdrop. But unlike the grey water in New York's harbor, the water in the Havana harbor is rich blue.

BUS EXCURSIONS

Havana is an exciting city, but sooner or later you'll want to visit other parts of Cuba. Nearby cities include Matanzas, the birthplace of rumba (to the east), or Pinar del Río (to the west). Another short trip takes you to the Viñales tobacco-growing region near Pinar with its unusual *mogotes* (flat-topped mountains) and caves. If you can tolerate a place that's off-limits to most Cubans but has beautiful beaches, Varadero is nearby, just east of Matanzas.

All of these near-to-Havana places are reachable by bus from the **Terminal de Omnibus Nacionales**, on Avenida Rancho Boyeros near Plaza de la Revolución, a few blocks southwest of Avenida Salvador Allende.

Foreigners are expected to pay for tickets in dollars. Entering the terminal, Cubans go straight ahead while foreigners turn into a hall to the right and enter a office with a blue wall, across from the cafeteria. One usually arrives a half-hour before departure time, which is often delayed. The ticketing clerk behind the desk will not sell you a ticket until she knows that your bus will indeed be departing.

Tickets are normally sold one-way rather than round-trip. As I was purchasing my ticket to Cárdenas for US$6 (while Cubans were only paying 6 pesos for theirs), a German tourist became outraged that he was not allowed to buy his ticket to Pinar del Río in Cuban pesos. He should have understood that Cubans are making US$20 a month while Europeans and North Americans visiting Cuba are making a hundred times as much for comparable jobs. The Cuban system of low salaries is compensated for by subsidized public transportation and housing, basic food necessities (a limited ration), and cultural events. Cubans are thus partially shielded from the free market. Foreigners coming from free market economies are expected to continue within their type of market in certain venues.

But foreigners have more than their fair (and fare) share of opportunities to use the Cuban subsidized economy. When I returned to Havana from a city called Cárdenas (see Chapter 9), ticketing agents were obligated to sell me my ticket for 6 Cuban pesos, since this non-tourist city did not supply its bus station with facilities to operate in the dollar economy.

For faster, more comfortable and more expensive excursion bus alternatives targeted to foreigners, ask in any hotel for the nearest Viazul bus station. This writer has traveled on both comfortable air-conditioned tourist buses and the regular excursion buses from the Terminal de Omnibus Nacionales, finding the latter trips more rewarding, at least for one who wishes to engage in conversation with Cubans during the trip.

A possible disadvantage of the regular Cuban excursion buses is that, because of scheduling systems and lengthier rides, an overnight stay even in nearby cities may become necessary.

RAILROADS

Cuba is the only Caribbean country with a functioning passenger railroad system. The traveler out of Havana has three alternatives. The **tren militar** is slow but runs more frequently and is the cheapest alternative. The **LADIS** train departs for locations east of Havana at 4:50 p.m. (check for schedule changes) and stops at major cities along the way until it reaches Santiago and Guantánamo in the early morning of the next day. The seats are large and comfortable, and each car has a very basic toilet room. This train looks like a partially-restored Old Havana on wheels. The **Especial**, usually with air conditioned cars (ask for car #6 to be sure) has its own schedule, which will probably change by the time you read these lines, so it's best to find out at the station.

The Estación Central of Havana.

To compare, the LADIS train costs US$3.50 to Matanzas, a two-hour plus trip covering 61 miles (98 km), sometimes taking longer, while the Especial costs US$10 to the same city, doing the trip in slightly faster time. The cheaper and more frequent tren militar is an electric train which lists a three-hour trip from Havana to Matanzas, but may take considerably longer, especially if an electrical outage occurs somewhere along your route. Each car of a LADIS train has its delightful *Ferromoza* (rail hostess) who invites travelers to consult her should they you have any questions or difficulties, and points out that there is a first-aid station on the train should anyone feel ill.

Railroad lovers will find train travel in Cuba enchanting. The **Estación Central** of Havana is conveniently located at the southernmost end of Old Havana, within easy walking distance of the Capitolio, on Avenida Bélgica (also known as Egido). At the LADIS office, a friendly and distinguished woman by the name of Daisy (who speaks impeccable English) will offer advice should you have any confusion about ticket service. While you're waiting for your train, you can admire at the station's 1842 Baltimore steam engine, the oldest in Latin America, painted in a deep, glossy red with black trim.

COCHES

Outside the bus terminal, impatient travelers can find drivers of *coches*, essentially long-distance collective taxis. In fact, if you look disturbed about your travel arrangements, these drivers will find you. You'll be charged according to the number of passengers the driver can hustle up. I was approached by the "agent" of one of these drivers with an offer of US$20 to Cárdenas in a full car, later lowered to US$15. I was promised that the traveling time would be cut in half. Compare this to the US$6 bus fare to the same city and the *coche* rates were not bad.

TAXIS

Within the city there are two kinds of taxis, those marked as such, usually more modern automobiles, and independent *coches*, generally more ancient cars. You can find these *coches* by flagging down older cars and asking for the rate to a particular place. Or you can find the usual street hustler outside hotels (with an official tourism ID) who can get you a car for a small tip. A few comparisons. From El Prado to the airport in a government-owned taxi will cost you US$17 plus tip, while one of these *coches* will cost you US$12 plus tip. An illegal hustler promised to get me a similar *coche* for US$10, but my allegiance to my regular "finder" was not worth breaking to save a couple of dollars.

Another comparison: from El Prado to the garden community of former mansions in Fifth Avenue in Miramar would cost US$8 in a modern taxi, but instead I had a bumpy ride in a 1951 Chevy with Pepe for only US$5. Some of these private car owners operate within the law and others are part of the underground economy. If your "finder" has an official ID, chances are your *coche* will be legit.

FOR FUN

Bicitaxis (pedaled by the driver) and **horse-and-buggies** are mainly for the atmosphere, but once in awhile when in a crunch, a carriage cyclist can get you from point A to point B for a U.S. dollar.

HITCHHIKING

Called *hacer botella*, hitchhiking was especially necessary during the height of the fuel crisis in the mid-1990s. You don't see as much hitchhiking nowadays except in the more remote rural regions, where government drivers are encouraged to pick up passengers. Government officials called *amarillos* (because of their yellow uniforms) are found in designated spots, often under bridges, organizing hitchhikers on a first-come-first-ride basis. Within Havana, an occasional frustrated commuter whose *camello* is stuck at an oasis may wave a thumb. Hitchhiking is not perceived as an adventuresome way to travel but rather as an occasional necessity. A foreigner who decided to hitchhike might be seen as odd by Cubans, who assume visitors from abroad have enough money for a *coche*.

CAR RENTAL

Car rental operations are easily found in major hotels, and are expensive (minimum US$50 per day with air conditioning). Renting a car can be a strategic alternative for seeing the country when sharing the cost, but it is senseless within Havana.

AIR TRAVEL

The shiny new red-white-and-blue **José Martí International Airport** in the southwest suburbs (financed with Canadian support) offers quick flights to Cuba's interior and is the primary international port of entry for foreign visitors. The least expensive alternative for getting to and from Havana is **Cubana de Aviación**. For example, if you use Cancún as a port of entry, Cubana's fares are 30 percent less than Mexicana's. **Sol Y Son**, Cubana's travel agency on the premises of the Cancún airport, does an efficient job in preparing tourist cards and hotel vouchers, and can usually get you out to Havana on the midday flight if you've arrived early enough in the morning. A flight to Santiago de Cuba is approximately US$170 round trip. The best thing about air travel out of Havana is that travelers can purchase a one-way ticket for not much more than half the round trip fare, and then work their way back to Havana by land.

GETTING AROUND AS THE CUBANS DO

Don't listen to the travel agent who offers to get you around without hassles in artificially-designed transportation systems unknown to most Cubans. Getting around Havana as the Cubans do is part of the adventure of this great city. During the mid-1990s, public transportation faced a grave crisis. Having experienced the public transportation system at various stages in the 1990s, I can testify that things are getting better.

Rumors from insiders suggest that the irreplaceable motors of some of the *camellos* are on their last legs. The loss of the *camellos* would mean the demise of one of the city's quirkiest landscape features. But with or without camels, getting around Havana is almost as fun as what awaits you at your destination.

Depending on Elegguá

The Afro-Cuban *orisha* (saint) of destiny is Elegguá, who is always dressed in red and black. The best way to get around in Havana is to leave it up to Elegguá, Lord of the Crossroads. Some words of advice by poet Tomás Burgos:

AGO ELEGGUÁ
by Tomás Burgos

A stone in the river at the crossroads
will show the way to my kingdom

A stone in the sea asks for the blood of roosters.
it's the house of Elegguá, the key to our destiny.
Show us the road, good stone.

21 possibilities,
21 paths in the light,

but if Elegguá does not fancy,
no gate will open.

He's the one tossing the dice
like an elder child
who deals out good fate and bad,
who engenders life
and engenders death.

Puerile gnome, wise and devilish,
moody and powerful father,
tell me how to forge my path
when the light gets lost,
how to arrive at truth through the shadows,
how to defy the obstacles
and the mocking witches of the night,
how to triumph over the obliterating magic
that ambushes our innocence.
Tell me, stone in the river,
sea shell of Elegguá,
how to topple the obstacles of fate.

Chapter Four

HOUSING:
The Search for Tenants

Foreigners entering Havana take note: housing searches for you,
you don't search for it. The best strategy for finding a place to
stay is to look like a foreigner. It's like walking through an outdoor bazaar and being summoned by ceramic or sweater vendors.
But here in Havana, walking down any street in the center of
town, you are summoned by cheerful people offering you a pleasant place to stay.

The legalization of homestays coupled with the absence of real estate agents means that people wishing to rent a room in their house must use creative methods to find you. Without the "help" of middlemen, these homestay hawkers revive a nostalgic anachronism from primitive capitalism. This is the best of all worlds: capitalism functioning in a freewheeling market in the midst of socialism that prevents middlemen and monopolies from artificially boosting prices. With Havana's reputation for cramped housing, it is truly amazing that so many Habaneros find a room in their houses to rent to a foreigner.

Who knows where the myth of overcrowded housing came from, but after having visited and stayed in numerous apartments in Havana, I can affirm that the average working-class Habanero has as much housing space in historic Havana as his counterparts in historic Paris or uptown Manhattan. According to Cuban researcher Patricia Rodríguez Alomá, "the average occupation per household [in Old Havana] is of 3.3 persons, with 0.9 persons per room and 1.9 persons per bedroom."

Cuba's low birth rate, the lowest in Latin America and on a par with that of the most developed nations, certainly alleviates the pressure on housing. For Cubans, most housing is heavily subsidized, and tenants are not supposed to be charged more than 10 percent of their salary for rent. Some housing has fallen through the cracks and entered the underground free market. New York and Parisian apartment dwellers, here's a line for your next cocktail party; a Cuban friend of mine lamented that "it's difficult to find an apartment in good condition for less than US$10 or US$15 a month."

Foreigners in Cuba will not become part of this Cuban housing market, unless they choose to live in quarters that are rented illegally with the "landlord" evading taxes. But with the legalization and subsequent abundance of legitimate homestays, it makes no sense to rent from an illegal landlord just to save a few dollars.

A few years ago, with a rash of illegal homestays becoming a main-stay of the underground economy, the Cuban government heeded the proverb "fewer laws make fewer offenders" and legalized (and taxed) the renting of rooms in Cuban homes.

The going rate for renting a room in a legal homestay is US$20 per night, but with such bazaar and bizarre competition, I've found good places available for only US$10 — or rather, the owners of these places found me. (On my most recent trip to Havana, I opted for a US$20 room with a full breakfast thrown in because the owners, Eduardo Milá and his friends, were en-gaging personalities.) Biweekly or monthly stays usually receive a discount.

A few Havana homestays shall be listed in this chapter, but it should be understood that if you look like a foreigner and stroll through central districts of Havana, housing will find you. If, mi-raculously, you've eluded the room-renters, just ask around in the neighborhood and the people will guide you.

Sometimes you'll find a whole apartment to yourself, as the owners will have moved in with family to liberate their apart-ment. One such single-bedroom apartment, offered for US$10 a day or US$200 a month, was comparable in size and amenities to the apartment we once rented in the Twentieth Arrondissement in Paris for US$1,000.

I've searched desperately for housing in Paris, Barcelona, New York, and Los Angeles, but housing has always searched obligingly for me in Havana. In Paris, Barcelona, New York, and Los Angeles, they were doing me a favor. In Havana, I was doing them a favor. When it comes to housing for foreign visitors, Viva La Habana!

BUYING AN APARTMENT

Viva La Habana, unless you are accustomed to suburban living with space and privacy. For such luxuries you will pay dearly in

Havana, and you'll be situated away from the action, so you'll have added transportation costs.

Yes, you are allowed to "buy" a house or apartment, but when it comes time to sell, you sell back to the government. The government real estate bureaucracy determines whether or not your property has increased in value, and how much. To make such a purchase, you must deal with what Cubans call an *inmobiliaria*. Havana's most important *inmobiliaria*, a joint government-private enterprise, is listed at the end of this chapter.

In 1999, Havana apartments were selling for US$1,450 per square meter (that's US dollars!), so a spacious 200-square-meter apartment near the ocean would cost US$290,000. By Parisian or Manhattan standards, that price seems reasonable, but in a country where workers earn less than US$20 a month, we're talking about ad hoc apartheid.

One Cuban Communist Party official confided with me: "I can't understand why a foreigner would come here and pay for an exorbitant inmobiliaria property when they can stay with a Cuban family for a tiny fraction of the cost and share the Cuban way of life."

HOTELS

It used to be that foreigners, especially those from the United States, would purchase three days of a hotel vouchers in order to have their hotel listed on their tourist card. They wanted to avoid a repetition of horror stories in which tourists arriving at the José Martí International Airport without hotel vouchers were being required to pay for three nights at a five-star hotel before they were allowed to enter the country.

On my next-to-last trip to Havana, I waited at the immigration cubicle, clutching my hotel vouchers in vain, for the immigration official had no desire to see them. He just looked down at my U.S. passport, smiled, and said, "Don't worry, I won't stamp

93

your passport." (In my case it made no difference since I had a license to travel legally to Cuba from the U.S. Department of Treasury, Foreign Assets Control. If you're a U.S. citizen, it means that some of your tax money went to pay for my license to travel to Cuba.)

On my most-recent visit, I simply didn't bother purchasing hotel vouchers but listed the name of a hotel on my tourist card. Again, the immigration official did not ask to see a voucher.

For the most recent housing requirements, travelers should ask for advice at their nearest Cuban consulate; travelers from the United States should contact the **Cuban Foreign Interests Section** in Washington, D.C. (tel: 202-797-8518) or **Marazul Tours** (tel: 800-223-5334).

The housing dilemma is resolved by staying in a hotel for a day or two while you wait for better housing to find you. If you're standing on any well-transited bus stop, an offer of a homestay will arrive before the bus does. I registered for one night in a hotel and before I'd seen my room, I was slipped the address of a nearby homestay by the chambermaid.

The hotel scene has normalized since the police crackdown, and the presence of hustlers and prostitutes around the hotels has diminished considerably. In some hotels, two or three women will sit together at a table in the cafeteria, order a fruit drink or beer, and wait. They might wink at you, but they are no longer propositioning, and they'll wait for their potential client to approach. The Cuban Revolution had once eliminated prostitution, which resurfaced during the depression of the 1990s. Perhaps they are on their way to discovering a new strategy for re-eliminating the world's oldest profession. Today, a father with his children in front of a Havana hotel will no longer be placed in a situation of having to respond to questions like:

"Daddy, what was that woman whispering to you?" or "Why did she take you by the arm."

The nearer you are to Havana when you make your hotel reservation, the lower the cost of your room. If you enter Havana from Cancún, Mexico, for example, Sol Y Son Tours, just across from the airport, will sell hotel vouchers for about 25 percent less than what they would be sold for through an agent in a far-off country. (See hotel suggestions at the end of this chapter.)

The most inexpensive hotels deal exclusively in Cuban pesos and they may or may not be allowed to let to foreigners. The facilities at these places are not necessarily up to Western standards (you may have to bring your own toilet paper) but they represent a slice of Cuban reality that is worth experiencing, if you can talk your way into a room for a night.

ALTERNATIVES

Government-run hotels are rather businesslike considering the friendliness of the country they represent. My subjective impression, based on anecdotal experience, is that hotels belonging to the **Islazul** chain are the most convivial, and the most likely to offer special monthly rates. If you can negotiate a monthly rate, an Islazul hotel might be a good place to live, in combination with taking meals in a nearby home (also for a monthly rate). Regular meal services are found by the hit-and-miss method of asking around.

In Havana, asking around is a superb strategy for finding what you are not looking for. The serendipity factor is one of the city's great assets. I once found a superb homestay because I was asking around for train information.

Talking to people in this manner may lead to a friendship and a subsequent invitation to stay in someone's apartment or home as a houseguest. In this scenario, the residents of the apartment will not ask you for any rent, but you should insist on their accepting some sort of appropriate gift and make a corresponding invitation.

Seasoned world travelers find Havana's legal homestay scene an exciting alternative to the more segregated housing options in other great cities. In the absence of brokers or middlemen, with no registration procedures, with no corporate solemnity, but with the exciting element of chance, the world of Havana's homestays has evolved into a nostalgic return to primitive capitalism under socialist guidelines. The traveler's freedom of choice is extraordinary.

First, tell the person who makes you the offer that you are looking only for a legal, taxpaying homestay. Then pay for a single night, if you wish, and if your experience is not optimal, simply return to the boulevard and allow another homestay to find you.

Business people may wonder whether this type of housing is in keeping with their social category. Every indication is that most Cubans who do business with you will respect you for avoiding "tourist apartheid." Doing business in Cuba requires getting to know the people and the culture. What better way to start then by staying in the home of Cubans!

A SHORT TOUR OF HAVANA HOUSING

Without resorting to encyclopedic lists, let's spot check some of Havana's housing alternatives, both in the inner city and on the beach front. These are places you'll probably miss if you depend on travel agents or taxi drivers. (All Havana phone numbers should be prefixed by 53-7.)

A Few Inspected Homestays

Only five blocks from Parque Central, on a narrow street in Centro Habana, Calle Aguila 103, at apartment 3, first floor (equivalent to the second floor for North Americans), the dynamic Zoraya Márquez offers a one-bedroom apartment for rent with complete privacy, a practical kitchen, air conditioning, and a view of the street from the cozy living room. Like many Centro Habana streets, Calle Aguila is very dark at night, but the street is well patrolled and the neighbors are friendly. This apartment is strategically located near shopping areas, Old Havana, and the Malecón. Write to Zoraya at: Apartado 2091, Habana 2, C.P. 10200, Cuba. Better yet, call her up (tel: 61-5185). Or, just ring doorbell #3. The going rate is US$20 per night, but Zoraya will listen to bargaining, especially if you're staying more than a few nights.

"I haven't had a tenant for awhile," Zoraya told me, with her smiling daughter at her side, "so you can have it for US$10 if you like."

Mr. Idalberto Córdoba Simón has rooms available within the shopping district of Centro Habana. Here, there is more privacy than with a typical homestay, a communal kitchen, and a shared living room with TV. The building is attractively painted on the outside, with tropical plants in the living room. Idalberto, who invited me to photograph the interiors of his pleasant house, can be reached by telephone at 63-0856. Clean and comfortable rooms go for US$25 but that rate goes down to US$20 if you stay three or more days.

97

This friendly man will rent you a room here in Centro Habana.

A block from the Malecón, at Calle Industria #8, apartment 4, between Genio and Refugio (only two blocks west of El Prado), Eduardo Milá rents a room within his pleasant balcony apartment. Eduardo wins my Gracious-Host Award, a great honor since there's a full field of competitors in Havana's graciousness race. Eduardo is a recent convert to Santería, proving you don't have to be black to practice an Afro-Cuban religion. His decision to become a *santero* came shortly after the Pope's visit, and he went through the obligatory year of wearing exclusively white garments, from head to foot.

Eduardo's friends are quite entertaining for those guests who wish to join them in the living room. But the tenant gets as much privacy as he wishes, with the guest bedroom next to the shared bathroom. Eduardo also serves a full breakfast with great Cuban coffee, and the package is US$20 a night. A monthly stay will earn you a considerable discount.

98

Once you get to know Eduardo and his friends, which won't take long, anxiety about the need for privacy will dissipate. You'll learn much about Havana from your host's congenial conversation. Mellow Eduardo talks softly but blasts his eclectic array of music, including hard-to-find collectors' items, including traditional Cuban boleros. His neighbors call him *el músico*, but he won't raise the volume before he gets your approval. My stay with these hosts left me with in-depth information about Santería, the history of Cuban music, university life, and the Cuban economy. A block away is a Copacabana-style outdoor nightclub with a one-dollar cover charge. No five-star hotel can compare culturally with this homestay, in a neighborhood swaying to the rhythms of rumba and Santería. Tel: 63-7605. Eduardo gave me two books on Cuban history as a going-away present.

Some visitors will prefer to do a Hemingway and live by the beach, 9 miles (15 km) to the east of Old Havana, making occasional day trips to downtown. Guanabo is a real Havana suburb, where beachcombers won't be isolated from Cuban reality. Only a block from the white sands and clear waters is Mr. Hugo Puig Roque's house, subdivided into three rental rooms, with Mr. Puig and his wife living on the premises. The rooms are quirky but comfortable, and there's a fair degree of privacy; a shady patio at the side of the house offers a place for resting, smoking a cigar, or chatting with other guests. Write to Hugo Puig Roque at: Calle 5ta Ave #47203, % 472 y 474, Guanabo, Ciudad Habana; you can also call him at 96-3426. Contrast Mr. Puig's house with resort hotels for US$150 a night, two kilometers west in Santa María del Mar.

Within the region of Playas del Este, Guanabo has the most democratic of beaches, with an array of snack shops and a few homespun *paladares* a block from the beach. All Cuban beaches are free to everyone, so the beachcomber can bike from Mr. Puig's house to nearby resort beaches.

These are a few examples from among Havana's abundance of homestays. For visitors who wish to become immersed in the culture and reality of Havana, no other housing option beats staying with local residents. Residential room rental only recently became legalized, so expect increasing competition. There are also homestays within the peso economy with lower rents.

Writing for a reservation in a home is ineffective, as mail service to Havana is irregular and slow. The best strategy is to arrive in the city, register at a hotel for a night, spend the day visiting potential homestays, accumulating visual imagery of the interiors of the city until you make your choice.

Selected Hotels

The refurbished **Caribbean Hotel** (US$33 per night), along El Prado, and the venerable **Deauville** (US$35 to US$40), right on the Malecón, are conveniently located with immediate access to the street-life between Centro and Old Havana, the Malecón, and Parque Central. To be right within Old Havana, in a district that resembles Le Marais in Paris, splurge on Hemingway's old (now-renovated) hotel, **Ambos Mundos** (US$59 to US$80). Or, one can relive scenes from *Fresa y Chocolate* by staying in Vedado, near the Coppelia ice cream parlor, at the basic **Hotel Colina** (US$30 to US$40) or the **St. Johns** (US$45 to US$50, with pool).

The most democratic beachside hotels are from the Islazul chain in Guanabo. Both the **Hotel Gran Via** and the **Villa Playa Hermosa** have friendly service, pools, live music, and moderately-priced restaurants, with rooms running for between US$21 and US$35.

Criteria for "low" and "high" season vary from hotel to hotel, with the lowest seasons in the winter and between March and April and the highest season between July and August. Prices listed above are for single occupancy, with the per-person cost decreasing by about a third with double occupancy.

I tracked down some budget tourists who began their stay in cheaper Havana hotels like the **Lido** (where you're more likely to find Cuban guests) but ultimately decided that a homestay would save money and improve the quality of life.

Anecdotal evidence suggests that the staff of Islazul chain hotels should be hired as consultants to the other chains in order to teach human warmth and friendly service. This opinion is based on crash visits to twenty-five different hotels. Reservations from abroad must be made through a travel agent specializing in Cuba, who will supply you with hotel options, and then vouchers for the one you choose.

Inmobiliarias for Purchasing Housing

Visitors with money to spare and who do not wish to deal with Cuba's intense public life may prefer to purchase their housing away from the crowds. Fine apartments are available for US$1,450 per square meter. Cubans believe these places are overpriced, but when the U.S. Congress lifts travel restrictions and tourists flood in from the United States, these apartments may turn out to be a worthy investment.

Contact **Real Inmobiliaria, S.A.** (tel: 249-871, 249-872, or 249-873; fax: 249-875) for real estate information. This company also has branches in Monaco and Italy. **Groupe J.P. Pastor,** in Monaco, can be reached by phone at (377) 93-30-37-37 or by fax at (377) 93-30-37-32. (The fact that these guys are located on the Cote d'Azur tells you something about the prices awaiting you.) In Rome, contact **Grupo Navarra** by phone at (396) 77-208-665 or by fax at (396) 77-206-105.

Havana's residents complain of an acute housing shortage, but you'd never know it by the persons-per-room statistics, the total absence of homeless people, and the availability of rooms in the apartments of Habaneros. Most Habaneros live in heavily subsidized apartments. Many local residents own their own homes

101

or apartments within socialist rules that do not allow for speculating with such properties. Foreigners in search of private properties are entering a heavily restricted market. New *inmobiliarias* are projected, but what will happen in the housing market when the embargo is lifted is unfathomable.

HOUSING FROM TOP TO BOTTOM

The bottom end of Havana's housing scenario, although it wouldn't qualify for the "American dream," seems superior to the bottom end of the rest of Latin America. A few pockets of "Palestinian" shantytowns are the only blemish at this level, and compared to the *favelas* of Río and the *vecindades* of Mexico City, one can safely say that Cuba's revolutionary government has been able to provide the basics for the least fortunate.

On the other hand, residents of Havana with professional degrees (the closest thing that comes to a middle class) live in quarters far more cramped than their counterparts, the middle-class minorities in other Latin American countries. Open-air balconies make these small apartments more liveable, and there's a consolation in that the streets, parks, taverns, ice cream parlors and seawall constitute a veritable public living room belonging to all the city's residents. Nevertheless, some Habanero professionals and intellectuals have expressed their frustration and sometimes anger that people who balked at struggling to earn a degree are out there making considerably more money in the tourism industry, and can thus afford more comfortable housing.

I passed on these frustrations to a Cuban official, who recognized the unfairness, while insisting that Havana has achieved a greater degree of housing equality than any other Latin American capital. He mentioned a program for encouraging tourism workers to voluntarily donate a portion of their tips to help improve the quality of life of Cubans who have no access to dollars.

The humanitarianism Cuba's housing system was tested during the Haitian refugee crisis. "It is ironic," wrote Drake University professor Jon Torgerson, "that Cuba gives shelter to Haitian refugees by placing them in scarce housing in Cuba, while our [U.S.] government puts Haitian refugees in crude camps on military bases also in Cuba!"

The Cuban government has been more successful in its housing programs than it has with food issues, as we shall explore in the next chapter.

FOOD:
The Epic Drama

DIET & DIEHARDS

For three decades, Cuba was the only country in Latin America to have eliminated hunger. Through a rationing system and a wage policy that prevented privileged Cubans from making more than five times as much as others, food distribution was relatively even. But it seems that everything right about food policy was also wrong. Cuba's diet was sustained through the massive importation of basic foods (mainly wheat and rice) from the Soviet bloc.

While Cuba was dependent on food imports, Soviet benefactors paying high prices for Cuban sugar made monocultural sugar exportation an expedient system — a system that was rooted, unfortunately, in the country's colonial heritage. Monocultural production of plantation crops like sugar, coffee, or cotton is a dead end when a nation strives for a sustainable food economy.

In the 1990s, when the U.S. embargo was stiffened and Cuba lost her overseas sources of food imports, fertilizers, and pesticides due to the Soviet collapse, the Cuban government was forced to pursue three related programs: (1) diversifying food production (a reasonable possibility); (2) transforming the entire agriculture system into an organic, rather than chemical-based, system (an unprecedented experiment); and (3) changing the basic dietary culture of the Cuban people, which had been based on a pervasive colonial heritage (a virtually impossible task).

Dietary reform, a touchy subject in any country, had a lot of potential in Cuba. What Cubans call *viandas* (roots like *yuca* and potato) were in fact just as nutritious as wheat, provided more fiber than white bread, and were much more suitable for growing in Cuba's soil and climate. Of all the government's nutrition measures, the substitution of *viandas* for grains in the national diet was the easiest to implement, especially since Cubans' distinct style of preparing *yuca* (with a large dose of healthy garlic) was tasty, nutritious, and within cultural norms. Likewise, potatoes were easy to popularize, although Cubans like their potatoes fried, which required scarce cooking oil or lard. Complaints of reduced rations often highlighted the scarcity of cooking oil, but Cubans were hardly open to the idea of preparing potatoes in a healthier, unfried fashion. (In fairness, my most memorable potato eating experiences took place when I was invited by Cuban families to dinners that included potatoes cooked with oil and garlic.)

More difficult than pushing *viandas* was convincing Cubans that vegetable proteins (especially soy), were healthier and just as tasty as animal proteins. To echo Liván's sentiments once more: "We feel we're not eating if we don't have meat as a part of our meal." Frenchmen, North Americans, and South Americans would resist just as stubbornly if their leaders attempted to get them to switch from beef to tofu. Cuban authorities have been pushing, literally, for a "middle ground"—ground beef product that blends

105

beef with soy. When I asked Habaneros about this highly publicized product, their responses ranged from suspicion to ridicule.

So restricted is the dietary heritage of Cuba's *criollo* regimen, that fish, a healthier alternative to beef and a more sustainable product than cattle, is often not consumed outside of fishing villages. (And when it is, it has to be fried.)

RITUAL CUISINE

To understand this country's limited variations in cuisine, one must simply quote the Cubans themselves. Carmen Alfonso Hernández's book *100 Questions and Answers About Cuba* (1996) does not even set aside a single category for food. Instead, Cuban food is introduced with the country's menu of mixed drinks. Within this short section, cocktails earn the same space as the food. Incredibly, for a country surrounded by ocean, fish is not even mentioned!

Cuba's national dish is referred to as *ajiaco criollo*, which includes meat (often pork cooked with bitter orange), a *vianda* (usually *yuca*, potato, or fried plantains), either *moros y cristianos* (steamed rice with black beans) or the *congrís* variation (fried rice with red beans and pork skins), and a fresh salad (almost always with the obligatory tomatoes and cucumbers). Cuban organic produce has a scintillating flavor, and salads are especially attractive when they include avocado. Chicken, usually fried, takes the place of the routine pork on occasion. (Fast food outlets serving fried chicken abound in Havana.)

Even the most confirmed health food addicts would be sorry to pass up the superb culinary experience of *chicharrón de cerdo* (crispy pork fried in its own grease). There's a saying in Spanish: *poco veneno no mata*, or "a little poison won't kill you." *Lechón* (suckling pig) is another pork delicacy. The basic *ajiaco criollo* is no better in upscale places than in a typical US$2 restaurant, but when it comes to *lechón*, you get what you pay for. The best *lechón* I've eaten was at an outdoor tourist restaurant at Cueva del Indio near the *mogotes* of Viñales, in the province of Pinar del Río. This is an easy day trip west of Havana. You eat next to a natural pool at the mouth of a cave, under a thatched roof. No guilt from diverging from my normally healthy diet, but there was an acrid aftertaste of tourist apartheid.

Two miracle ingredients spice up Cuban cuisine: garlic and bitter orange. What makes Cuba's basic diet worth the repetitiveness (for both taste and nutritional reasons), is the liberal use of garlic. Try the fiber-rich *yuca* without garlic and you'll wonder where the taste is. Then eat it Cuban style, with garlic, and it becomes a delicacy. Bitter orange lends grilled pork a wonderfully fragrant flavor that's also worth indulging in regularly.

When black beans are combined with rice, even white rice, the protein yield is increased. A vegetarian who tolerates cooking oil would appreciate a meal of black beans with rice, *yuca* in garlic, *tostones* (crispy, fried, green banana chips), and a tomato-cucumber-avocado salad, washed down with a fresh fruit drink.

I've eaten twice with Cubans in Havana's Chinatown, and you'd think that they'd take advantage of the opportunity to escape their daily rice. Yet they still go with the rice (usually a fried rice dish with vegetables) instead of Chinatown's variety of vegetable dishes cooked in soy.

Vegetarians

Havana's first organic vegetarian restaurant, **El Bambú**, is a major attraction of the Jardín Botánico in Arroyo Naranjo. You may get away with paying in Cuban pesos if you buy a lunch reservation at the entrance to the park. Other vegetarian restaurants are projected, and by the time you read these lines, a revolutionary ecological restaurant in the **Bosque de la Habana** along the cleaned-up Rio Almendares may be ready. Restaurants aside, once you get to know your neighbors, you'll find Cuban women who will prepare vegetarian dishes for a reasonable price in their homes.

EATING OUT

Since tourism escalated in Cuba in the 1990s, the restaurant scene
has evolved unpredictably. Tour guides of the 1990s advised visitors to limit themselves to so-called dollar restaurants with Euro-
prices too expensive for Cubans. The same old Hemingway nostalgia hangouts, the overpriced **La Bodeguita del Medio** (near
the Plaza de la Catedral) and **El Floridita** (at the edge of Old
Havana near Parque Central), were obligatory stops.

When family-run businesses were legalized, the *paladar*
(roughly translated as "place of good taste") sprouted up within
homes and apartments. By 1997, government-run Cuban restaurants were losing ground to the more quaint and economical
paladares. But the same laws that made the family-run, homecook-
ing *paladar* an attractive alternative to restaurants (limitations in
numbers of tables, prohibition against hiring non-family employees) would limit its options in competing with the restaurants. By
late 1997, new restaurants were springing up, in the image of what
had already existed in Chinatown, with a basic *criollo* meal costing
about two dollars.

In 1999, while researching for this book, I ate at various
paladares and compared them with economy restaurants like the
charming **Hanoi** in Old Havana (Brasil Street) and the ones in
Centro Habana's Chinatown. A few *paladares* like **Doña Blanquita**
(Prado 153) and **Doña Nieves** in Vedado (Calle 19 between 2
and 4) were probably worth the extra cost, but the newer homespun and less-gentrified restaurants were comparable in both food
and atmosphere.

Culinary adventure awaits you in non-tourist neighborhoods,
where unique restaurants and *paladares* dish out home-cooked food.
The people in the neighborhood will steer you to these hidden
eating surprises. The food is mainly *criollo*, but you'll find home
cooking with creative nuances, as I did in Regla, Arroyo Naranjo,
and Guanabo.

When splurging in a tourist restaurant, you might as well order what you can't find in neighborhood eateries: lobster and other seafood, plus Cuba's more moist version of Spanish paella, *arroz con pollo*. On the opposite end of the eating spectrum, with more adventure and less ambiance, are the peso-economy food stands scattered throughout Centro Habana and other non-touristy neighborhoods.

The Snack Route

Considering the roughly 20-peso-per-dollar exchange rate, you can stroll and eat, eat and stroll, and continue strolling and eating across the whole city and then return home with almost as much money as you left with. It might appear that a slice of pizza costs five or six dollars, but that $ sign is for pesos. Sandwiches are as low as two or three Cuban pesos. Soft drinks go for a peso. The same hearty Cuban coffee that costs a dollar or more in hotel restaurants goes for just a peso at makeshift stands and foodbars. Ice cream for three pesos, with almost every brand just as good as Coppelia. Roasted peanuts from street vendors for a peso. And Cuban pastries like the creamy *señorita* for a few pesos.

An ideal snack route begins in Centro Habana on the Malecón. Walk south on Avenida Italia (also known as Galiano). Turn right on Reina, which becomes Avenida Salvador Allende. Passing into Vedado, the name of the street changes to Carlos III and Zapata. By now you've had all you can indulge in for a lifetime. This tour ends at the Colón Cemetery. (If you're still alive by now, you can return via the same route and engage in a shopping binge, with supermarkets, department stores, a new shopping mall, and outdoor flea markets.)

WHEN EATING OUT GETS TIRESOME

Sooner or later, foreigners in Havana will be ready to settle down to a more normal life, which includes the type of balanced and

Farmers' market vendors.

healthy diet you can only get when you cater for yourself. As a starter, virtually every neighborhood has its own **farmers' market**, known as *mercado agropecuario* or *agromercado*. The granddaddy of these markets is found in Chinatown. Fresh fruit and vegetables, when in season, are available for prices which seem unbelievably cheap to foreigners (e.g., two oranges or bananas for a peso is equivalent to 40 pieces of fruit for a dollar!). Meat products are not as economical, so Cuba's food economy favors the vegetarian. But to Cubans, vegetarians are more foreign than North Americans, Mexicans, or Swedes.

To further cut "peso food" costs, the Ministry of Agriculture has encouraged and helped organize *organopónicos*, or urban agriculture gardens and fields that nullify the usual country-to-city transportation costs.

For whatever you can't find at the farmers' markets, check out the dollar supermarkets on main avenues in Vedado or Centro Habana. Scattered throughout the city are butcher shops and bakeries, in both the peso and dollar economy. More expensive convenience stores take dollars.

110

The *bodegas*, part of the national ration card system (where the local peso suddenly acquires real buying power), are only available to Cuban citizens. By western standards, these are "free stores" with only symbolic costs. Rations became severely limited during the economic crisis of the 1990s.

Budgets and Bartering

Home economists will be interested in tallying the cost of a monthly food budget in order to gauge the spending power of the roughly 50 percent of Cubans with no access to dollars who earn the peso equivalent of US$10 to US$15 dollars a month. Rent is 10 percent of the salary; bus and ferry transportation amounts to less than US$2 per month; medical care is free; culture, sports and entertainment are either free of charge or cost a peso; rationed clothing and footwear costs are minimal; and rationed food, also for symbolic costs, lasts about a week of every month. The average Cuban without dollar revenue is left with about US$5 to US$6 for the rest of the month's food budget.

The primary budgetary dilemma is food. Even a takeout meal with a large portion of pork, *vianda*, *congris*, and a tomato-cucumber-lettuce salad at the corner takeout place at Aguacate and Chacón in Old Havana costs 20 pesos (US$1), representing a considerable expense for the basic Cuban salary.

The answer, pushed in the mid-'80s, is urban agriculture in neighborhood or family gardens. (You can occasionally hear egg-laying hens squawking behind the facades of urban streets.) Another answer is to barter. Maribelle, a nursery school teacher, buses to the country on Saturdays to exchange salt for produce from farmers. Nonsmoking vegetarians who eat unfried food will do well in the bartering game, exchanging their cooking oil, pork, and cigarette rations for soy yogurt, breads, and produce. But since the 1990 fall of the Soviet bloc and the tightening of the U.S. economic embargo, those Cubans who maintain their colonial dietary heritage have been obligated to *resolver* (find creative ways to stay afloat). Ironically, some visiting foreign doctors hypothesize that the meager ration of red meat in the average Cuban's diet (coupled with the widespread use of bicycles as private transportation) has contributed to a high level of cardiovascular health.

As Cuba's economy inexorably improves, it becomes easier to *resolver*. But an unresolvable contradiction emerges when the island's virtually moneyless internal economy is overwhelmed by the tidal wave of the all-encompassing global economy. Part of this global incursion is an international restaurant scene and the dollar food stores, which are beyond the budgets of Cubans who do not receive generous gifts from relatives abroad.

Commenting to me on this situation, one government official was remarkably candid. "We tend to see things in extremes," he said. "Our vision of equality meant the exact same rations for all Cubans. But some Cubans are today better off than others, and we must find a way to provide more rations for those who have less."

FOOD RESCUE

Cuba's massive transformation to organic agriculture accompanied by a government-monitored network of private farmers was intended to rescue the country from the brink of famine.

In the so-called global economy, Cuba was left to fend for herself. The emergence in 1994 of *agromercados* was the medium for this rescue attempt. Unlike the dollar stores, the *agromercados* provided a variety of produce and collateral food items within the peso economy, with many items priced economically enough so that Cubans could complement their restricted *bodega* rations. The *bodegas* are open to Cubans only and the dollar stores, because of their high prices, offer very limited benefits to the population at large. The farmers' markets, on the other hand, are accessible to everyone in Havana, Cubans and foreigners alike.

The farmers' markets (there are at least 135 across the country) illustrate Cuba's food drama of epic proportions. They were first introduced when many Cubans were at the point of losing all hope for survival. While other Latin American countries were depending on U.S. food subsidies, the Cuban Democracy Act, passed by U.S. Congress in 1992, cut off food shipments that Cuba used to buy through foreign subsidiaries of U.S. corporations. If the success of the U.S. economic embargo could be measured by the degree of suffering of a people, then Congress and the Cuban exile lobby groups must have been gloating. U.S. newspaper pundits and book-writing experts regularly predicted the imminent fall of Fidel Castro and Cuba's socialist system.

Cuba's only possibility for survival was to call upon an immense pool of human resources, the product of an education system that had produced, in a country with only 2 percent of Latin America's population, 11 percent of Latin America's scientists.

Prior to 1990, approximately 80 percent of Cuba's farm production was state-run. Today, 73 percent of farming is independent of the state, with small private growers, and various forms of

113

co-ops (including "basic production units") taking up the slack. This transformation triggered the farmers' markets. As a result of the new forms of competition, state farms were obligated to take measures to increase their efficiency.

What appeared to be a remarkable rebirth in Cuba's food production was soon stricken with alarming contortions, the augury of a tragic miscarriage. Cuba's food rebound faced a triple assault: the 1996 Helms-Burton Act, Hurricane Lili (which also struck in 1996), and a major drought in 1998. But new farmers' markets continued to emerge. The *agromercados* became a symbol of the symbiosis between private enterprise and socialism. The hardships of the Special Period had threatened to obliterate the food ration system. But tax revenue from independent farmers was directed to keep the food ration system afloat.

The incursion of tourism and the dollar economy it ushered in could have flooded out the Cuban peso. Cubans with only pesos in their pockets saw dollar stores that were off-limits to them and began to doubt the validity of their own currency. But the farmers' markets, operating exclusively in Cuban pesos, became one of the mainstays of the peso economy, and restored a significant degree of the value of Cuban peso salaries.

With the embargo persisting at the turn of the century, Cuba's farmers' markets have become the symbol of a people that overcame a dramatic food crisis. Visitors planning on transcending a tourist perspective of Havana and becoming part of the fabric of daily life will do well to patronize and enjoy the *mercados agropecuarios*. Sooner or later, the dietary limitations of restaurant dining will take their toll, and even visitors who continue to enjoy the restaurant scene will want to add a healthy dietary complement of fresh fruits, vegetables, and other goodies available for very reasonable prices in Havana's farmers' markets. Many farmers' markets are not clearly marked, so the following list with markets and their locations will be especially useful. Proximity to a farmers' market may be an important factor in choosing one's place of residence.

Mercados agropecuarios (Farmers' markets)

- **Mercado Unico de 4 Caminos**, Calle Monte and Matadero. One of the most active of the farmers markets.
- **Egido y Zulueta**, near the Estación Central (railroad terminal).
- **Compostela y Sol**, Old Havana. Near the old Colegio de Belen.
- **Barrio Chino** (Chinatown), Zanja and Dragones, Centro Habana.
- **San Nicolas and Trocadero**, Centro Habana.
- **Colina and 10 de Octubre**, Santos Suárez, Municipio 10 de Octubre.
- **Monaco and Calle Mayia Rodríguez**, Víbora, Municipio 10 de Octubre.
- **La Palma**, Municipio Arroyo Naranjo.
- **Calle 8va and Tejar**, Lawton, Municipio 10 de Octubre.
- **Vía Blanca and Colina**, in front of the Ciudad Deportiva, Cerro.
- **Plaza de Marianao**, 51 y 124, Municipio Marianao. Old and spacious building in the style of the 4 Caminos Plaza.
- **51 and 88**, Marianao.
- **17 and G**, Vedado, Municipio Plaza.
- **41 and 41**, Municipio Playa.
- **190 and 51**, Municipio La Lisa.
- **Calzada del Cerro y Calzada de Palatino**, Municipio Cerro.
- **Santiago de las Vegas**, Municipio Boyeros.

Keep an eye out . . . As the food situation continues to improve, other farmers markets will be sprouting up.

CHAPTER SIX

DOLLARS AND PESOS:
Shopping, Banking, Health Care, and Other Transactions

BACK TO THE GOOD OLD DAYS

Imagine a department store without a parking lot beneath it or around it. Try to remember the days when the person attending to you from behind the counter was the owner of the store and not an employee. Picture a country whose banks are a recent invention, with personalized service that goes back to the Wells-Fargo days. Imagine a city in which every other citizen has something to sell you, with negotiable prices.

Now let's add a bit of drama to this quaint scenario. We find a historical clash between two radically different tiers of a rapidly evolving economy. On one level, there are dollar stores with Euro-pricing; on another, Cuban peso enterprises whose minimal prices are derived from an economy in which money was a virtual non-factor. Now add the human element to this clash. Cubans who receive dollars from relatives abroad or from tips in the tourism industry participate in the upper tier of the economy but also benefit from the lower tier. Cubans who do not receive dollars from foreign sources (roughly half the population) do their business as best they can, almost exclusively on the lower tier.

The reality of a two-tiered system of commerce is nothing new to Latin America. But in other Latin American countries, the population has been conditioned to accept class differences as a normal development of humanity. In Cuba, on the other hand, the population has been schooled on the idea of equality. Many Cubans without dollars view this two-tiered economy as unfair. Today's Cuban refugees are not escaping from the egalitarian woes of socialism but from the class differences of capitalism.

Ricardo Alarcón, president of the National Assembly of People's Power, has remarked, "While it is true that we have some things in our reality that are not to our liking—the dual economy, the circulation of dollars—that was done out of necessity. But it is something that we should try to eliminate, the sooner the better."

Off the record, another Cuban official admitted to me that the situation was far from ideal, and that the government was betting on an improving economy to eliminate the malcontent. But Arnulfo, a new type of Cuban abroad who travels back to his beloved country at least once a year, told this reporter that, "I left Cuba because I couldn't bear to see the bitterness of those who do not have access to dollars."

Arnulfo was a member of the Communist Party and decided to live elsewhere because of this diminishing of equality. One would

117

think that party members would live with certain privileges, but according to a doctor friend who travels frequently to Cuba, "Those who suffer the most are the militant revolutionaries who would not receive dollars because of the stigma attached to betraying their system. They watch their non-ideological neighbors gain comparative wealth thanks to gifts received from relatives in Miami."

It must be emphasized at this point that Cuba remains a much more egalitarian society than her Latin American neighbors. The human dissonance emerges because Cubans were taught to have such high standards of equality.

The foreign visitor steps into this system with certain constraints. There is a social pressure to not live at a different level from the majority of Cubans. The foreigner needs no invitation to join the exclusive consumer society thanks to his or her earnings from abroad. But to enjoy too many consumer goods from dollar stores will isolate the foreigner from the Cuban way of life. One is almost obligated to refrain from the commodity lifestyle that is normal only 90 miles to the north of Cuba and prevalent among the elites to the west of the Gulf of Mexico. Flaunting wealth in Cuba will not win friends or influence people.

This is the scenario in which the visitor to Havana enters into daily commerce. Such a dilemma is not necessarily unique to Cuba. I recall the French businessman who owned an expensive Mercedes and an older, cheaper Renault. His mechanic asked him why he drove the Renault to work instead of the Mercedes. The businessman responded that his rapport with his employees improves when he is not perceived as being different.

SHOPPING

Enter one of Havana's many department stores and you'll find the prices of most items to be no different than what they'd be in North America, although perhaps less expensive than in other

Caribbean countries. A similar situation is found in hotel stores, although prices are even higher at these venues since they cater to tourists only. The city's largest department stores are **La Época**, **Almacenes Ultra**, and the modern, mall-like **La Tienda de Carlos III**. The most popular shopping corridors are located on Obispo Street in Old Havana; in Centro Habana along Avenida Salvador Allende (where you'll want to enter La Tienda de Carlos III) and extending as far east as Avenida Reina, and then north on Galiano (where you'll find La Época); and along 23rd Street in Vedado, just north of the University of Havana.

La Época, in Centro Habana, one of Havana's most popular department stores.

Bargain hunting in one of Havana's flea markets.

Smaller **specialty or variety stores** still retain the Cuban custom of only letting in a certain number of people at a time. There will be lines outside these stores at prime-time hours. As one customer leaves, the guard lets the next customer in. Prices in these government-run stores may be either in Cuban pesos or dollars but they are lower than what you'd pay for the same item in a department store or at a sleek, new mall. These smaller stores are more likely found in the same shopping corridors mentioned above, as well as along Máximo Gómez between Centro Habana and Cerro.

Even lower prices are found at **outdoor flea markets**. Here, individual stalls are owned by Havana residents, so you do business directly with the proprietor. Many of the same types of items found in larger stores can be obtained in these outdoor markets for a lower price, and shopping is more fun. It is here where the Cuban government has worked out a friendly balance between capitalism and socialism. Businesses must be run by the owners themselves, and independent Cuban business people cannot hire employees. The result is a 19th century shopping ambiance. The best flea markets are found in Centro Habana, in particular just south of Chinatown crossing Reina.

Yet another tier of the shopping scenario is what is sometimes called the "black market" but more aptly named the "informal economy." This includes products like cigars, rum, and other factory discards that Cuban workers sell on the streets or from their apartments. Vendors will only hawk two or three popular products, but if you tell the vendor what you need, he may be able to obtain it for you. On this informal tier of the commerce scenario, bartering is also practiced by many Habaneros.

The shopping scenarios mentioned above generally serve one's daily living needs. Tourist shops will find you before you find them if you walk anywhere within Old Havana or in the vicinity of Parque Central. Stroll north or south on Calle Cuba in Old Havana for some of the city's best boutiques and arts-and-crafts shops.

BANKING AND MONEY EXCHANGE

The main difference between exchanging money in the black market and at the **Casas de Cambio** (CADECA Exchange Houses) is the possibility that you might have to wait on line at CADECA. There may be a one peso difference in exchange, or no difference at all. The exchange is approximately 20 pesos to the dollar. If it's too late at night to walk to CADECA, I can simply knock on the door of a friendly neighbor who will give me pesos for dollars, at the same rate as CADECA. He must be wagering that the value of the dollar will go up, but the dollar actually slumped from 1:22 to 1:20 during the year-and-a-half period between the Pope's visit and the Spring of 1999, so my neighbor is running a loss, unless he resells the dollars somewhere else for a higher price.

121

Like other Havana business establishments, CADECA runs its operation in a homespun and personal way. You wait on a line chatting or people watching, and as soon as the previous client leaves a special room with a money changer, the next person is guided personally by a guard into the exchange room.

Havana's first private bank, **Banco Financiero Internacional, S.A.** (at Calle Línea, near the Malecón, just west of the Hotel Nacional in Vedado) was founded in 1984. Cubans and foreigners alike may open accounts here with a choice of currency. This bank has branches in many of the important capital cities of the world. (Mailing address: Apartado 4068, Vedado, La Habana). Havana's first foreign bank, **Banco Caribeño de Holanda**, was opened in 1994, and at this writing there are at least twenty different foreign banks doing business in the city.

I've gotten friendly service at **Banco Internacional de Comercio**, on El Prado, about five blocks from the Malecón. All you need is a valid passport to open an old-fashioned savings account. Credit card withdrawals can be made at any Cuban bank. Cuban banking is pretty simple, without the myriad of different types of accounts for different purposes. I asked the officer at Banco Internacional de Comercio about opening a business account and she was not sure what that meant. There was no problem, she explained, for an account holder to deposit or cash foreign checks, cash travelers' checks, or withdraw money from credit cards like MasterCard, Diners Club and Visa. Plastic money is accepted at more modernized business establishments. The big exception, until the trade embargo is lifted, involves credit cards issued by U.S. banks, which are worthless in Cuba.

One Habanero friend tells me there's not much incentive for him to hold a savings account since interest rates are so low. "In the 1980s," he said, "when the peso had more buying power, the accumulated interest made a difference. Today, you might as well keep your money under your mattress."

The government is currently devising a system for cash loans. Usury had been frowned upon by the leaders of the Revolution, but today's economic evolution is going to require a lending system. At this writing, one can acquire a loan in the form of bonds that are earmarked for a specific purchase, with collateral coming from one's labor union or professional association.

Cuba's economy is changing as fast as the countryside viewed through the window of a speeding train, so the best advice for the potential visitor is to get briefed on the latest developments at the nearest Cuban consulate before traveling to Havana.

HEALTH CARE

Before traveling to Cuba, meet with your health insurance agent and demand to go over each and every possible loophole in your coverage abroad. The government organization **Asistur** (Asistencia al Turista) will assume any medical costs you may have once their representative sees you have international insurance coverage. Asistur is located on El Prado #254 between Old Havana and Centro Habana, between Animas and Trocadero. (Asistur's 24-hour hot-line numbers: 62-5519, 63-8284, or 33-8527.)

Tourist hotels, intercity trains, and other establishments have free first-aid stations, and in the case of an emergency, foreigners can expect to receive free treatment. An initial visit to a Cuban polyclinic is free. Otherwise, expect to pay for your health care, and just in case, carry evidence of proof that you will be able to afford any sudden but non-emergency care that you require.

Should you be planning a long stay in Havana through an international nongovernmental organization, your NGO should consult with your nearest Cuban consulate on the up-to-the-minute developments involving the modality for foreigners' payment for Cuban health insurance.

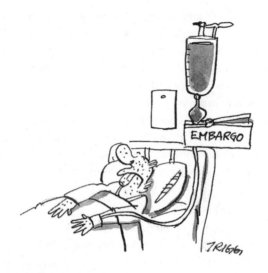

Medication Issues

Should you have a health condition that may need a specific medication, before traveling to Cuba contact the **American Association for World Health (AAWH)** for a list of medicines and drugs patented since 1980 which Cuba cannot freely purchase because of the U.S. trade embargo. (Address: 1825 K St., Suite 1208, Washington, DC 20006; tel: 202-466-5883.) The 1992 Cuban Democracy Act imposed a ban on subsidiary trade with Cuba. Recent corporate buyouts and mergers between major U.S. and European pharmaceutical companies mean that, for example, a Swedish pharmaceutical company that formerly traded with Cuba is no longer allowed to do so if partnered with a U.S. corporation.

"A humanitarian catastrophe has been averted," according to the AAWH, "because the Cuban government has maintained a high level of budgetary support for a health care system designed to deliver primary and preventive health care to all of its citizens. The inclusion of food and medicine in an international trade embargo is a violation of international human rights conventions which uphold the principle of free flow of food and medicines, even in wartime, to serve the basic needs of civilian populations."

Cuba does produce many of its own medicines, but you don't want to find out at the last minute that precisely the drug you need is not available because of the embargo. For example, Vascor, a calcium channel blocker produced by R.W. Johnson for heart patients, cannot be purchased by Cuban hospitals. Nor can Felbatol, a tablet used to prevent and control of epileptic seizures, produced by Carter-Wallace, Inc. and patented in 1990.

"The human consequences [of the embargo] are all too evident in the wards of Cuban hospitals," according to the AAWH. "When the AAWH delegation visited the cancer ward at the Juan Manuel Marquez Pediatric Hospital in Havana, our doctors found that oncologists do not have access to U.S.-manufactured cell-site-ports for chemotherapy." AAWH representatives observed unnecessary pain and suffering among children because of the unavailability of the cell-site port Implantofix, whose German and Swedish suppliers of the product are now prohibited from doing business with Cuba because they are associated with Braun Medical, Inc., based in Pennsylvania.

Health Tourism
Nevertheless, "Cuba's health care system is uniformly considered the preeminent model in the Third World," according to the AAWH. Should your own condition be parallel with a Cuban health care specialty, you would become a candidate for what is referred to as health tourism. Some of these specialties include: skin disorders like vitiligo, psoriasis and alopecia (treated with melagenina, a product derived from the human placenta); retinosis; pigmentaria; certain gerontological disorders; transplants of the heart, lung and pancreas; ophthalmological disorders; nervous system transplants; diabetes; orthopedic disorders; stomach problems; and drug-abuse treatment. Using DNA recombinant tech-

nology, Cuban scientists developed streptokinase for dissolving blood clots and a skin growth factor used to treat burn patients. Cuba also manufactures monoclonal antibodies that prevent organ rejection in kidney transplants. One of Cuba's most heavily marketed and successful products is PPG, an anti-cholesterol medicine derived from sugar cane, with a touted side effect of enhancing sexual prowess.

The various hospitals and clinics that provide treatment for such specialties within Cuba's medical establishment fall under the umbrella of **SERVIMED**. SERVIMED is located on Calle 18, No. 4304 between 43 and 47 in Playa. Tel: 33-2658 or 33-2023; fax: 33-2948. Cuba earns more than US$25 million a year from this health tourism, and its capitalist pharmaceutical exports help finance its socialist family doctor system.

"Cuban medical care in some fields like orthopedics is better than in the rest of Latin America," says Ciro de Quadors, a Brazilian physician working for the Pan American Health Organization in Washington, D.C.

Overseas sales of Cuban biomedical products exceed US$135 million annually, while Cubans may need to scrounge for simple things like aspirins and asthma inhalers. Within the health care scenario, one finds the same wobbly juxtaposition of capitalist and socialist economies. Although all Cubans, regardless of their economic situation, qualify for free heart transplants and other esoteric health treatment, some health tourism facilities are off-limits to Cubans. For the health consumer from abroad, Cuba may be the ideal setting for treatment and therapy, or it may be better to stay home, depending on the nature of one's medical condition.

Doctors and Clinics

Cuba's physician-to-population ratio is 1 to 255, as compared with 1 to 430 in the United States. One edge of Cuba's health care system may be considered avant-garde, but on the other edge, it's back to the good old days, with the friendly family doctor (earning a subsistence income) who knows everyone in the community and lives on the second floor of the neighborhood clinic. And like the good old days, Cuban family doctors often resort to "green medicine," derived from traditionally used herbs and other plant materials. This is not by choice, but in order to compensate for medicines not available because of the trade embargo.

The best source for hard-to-get medicines is the **Cira García Clinic**, at Calle 20, 4101, on the corner of 41st in Miramar (tel: 24-2811 through 24-2814). Payment is in dollars, and this is also a setting for emergency medical or dental treatment. The **Camilo Cienfuegos Pharmacy**, at L and 13 in Vedado (tel: 33-3599) is another source for exotic pharmaceuticals.

COMMERCE AND CULTURE

Visitors used to doing commerce by mail or phone will be in for a culture shock. Commerce in Havana is still an in-person affair, as it is in most Latin American countries. This may sound like an inefficient system, but once you get re-accustomed to dealing with human beings and budget your time well, this is a much less alienating way to engage in transactions.

ADDENDA:
OTHER USEFUL TRANSACTIONS

- **International telegraphs**. Try the **Ministerio de Comunicaciones**, on Ave Rancho Boyeros between 19 de Mayo and 20 de Mayo, Plaza de la Revolución.
- **Faxes**. All four- and five-star hotels offer the use of international fax machines and phones for prices equivalent to what we'd pay in North America or Europe.
- **Photo developing**. Vedado is the best district for locating photo shops. I've been to **Photoservice**, on Calle 23, corner of P, and received friendly help with a jammed camera. Also try

127

Publifoto, at Edificio Focsa, Calle M between 17 and 19. Many large hotels offer photo service.

- **Bookstores**. Outdoor bookstands around the cathedral square and on Obispo Street in Old Havana (La Internacional, Obispo 528) offer attractive book-buying opportunities. For collectors and historians, old issues of Cuban magazines and obscure or classic books can be found in any of Havana's intriguing used-book stores. Check out the south side of Colón, a block west of El Prado.

- **Post Offices**. There's a post office At Oficios 102 in Old Havana, and most neighborhoods have outdoor postal stands. **Warning:** do not depend on the mail service for important business. It may take as long as six weeks for letters to arrive from abroad, and sometimes they never arrive. Tell friends to send letters certified with a request for proof of receipt. Postal service is much more reliable if you purchase a P.O. Box, called *apartado postal*. Postal facilities are also found in luxury hotels.

Chapter Seven

THE BUREAUCRATIC NIGHTMARE

EXPECTING ENTANGLEMENTS?

Cuban film satires of government bureaucrats gave me hope that I could stumble into a bureaucratic nightmare of my own that would make for good reading. Rent the film *Guantanamera*, directed by the late Tomás Gutiérrez Alea and his partner Juan Carlos Tabío, and you will lust for a spicy engagement with the Cuban bureaucracy.

IMMIGRATION

Travel Restrictions for U.S. Citizens

My first potential for a good story was the chance of being rejected for a license to travel to Cuba by the **Office of Foreign Assets Control (OFAC)**, U.S. Department of the Treasury, 1500 Pennsylvania Avenue NW, Annex Building, 2nd Floor, Washington, D.C. 20220 (tel: 202-622-2480; fax: 202-622-1657). Surely such a long and unwieldy address increased my chances for a bureaucratic mishap.

But there are so many categories within which a U.S. citizen can indeed travel to Cuba that I am regularly approved for a license. Actually, the license allows you to spend up to US$100 a day in Cuba, not including airfare; it is not travel to Cuba but spending money there that is illegal. Travel license categories (brackets reflect this writer's opinions), include: government employees traveling on official business [like covert C.I.A. agents]; journalists employed by a news organization [the ones who covered the Pope's 1998 visit and saw their stories killed because of Monica Lewinsky]; fully-hosted travelers [virtually impossible, for even Fidel can't afford to pay your rent]; persons traveling to visit close relatives for humanitarian purposes [like taking an air conditioner to your cousin's steamy apartment]; persons engaging in professional, noncommercial research [comparing Cuban ice cream to the "31 flavors"]; persons traveling for freelance journalism [get a letter from your community newspaper]; persons traveling for clearly defined educational purposes [like studying coral reefs or learning to dance salsa]; persons traveling for human rights organizations [NRA reps compiling a report on Cuba's dictatorial prohibition of gun ownership]; persons traveling for purposes of import/export/transmission of information [to let Cubans know that we have the democratic right to choose the toppings for our hamburger served at Burger King].

Tourist Visas

Once I'd gotten my license, I hoped there would be problems obtaining a Cuban visa, which is really a tourist card that must accompany a valid passport. One picks up a tourist visa at any Cuban consulate (US$20) or at a travel agency specializing in Cuba (US$25). Hoping to confront a memorable bureaucratic challenge on my first trip to Havana, I waited until arriving at Cancún, Mexico, where I expected to be denied a visa. (I would have to find a raft heading to Cuba in the Gulf of Mexico and would pass *balseros* going in the opposite direction . . .) Unfortunately, right at the airport was **Sol Y Son Tours**, associated with Cubana de Aviación. Upon presenting my passport, I was immediately issued my tourist card, and they found space for me on a cheap flight two hours later.

Warning/*Cuidado!* Freelance journalists applying for a special journalist visa, even if they are Nobel prize winners (if not supported by a major news organization), will be wasting their time. Such applications are not processed by the Cuban consulate and must be sent to Havana, where they will languish. Better to simply go as a tourist.

Warning/*Cuidado!* Those who wish to apply for residency, if not supported by a project with a nongovernmental organization (NGO) or registering to study at a Cuban university, would do better to first travel to Cuba with a tourist visa for up to a month, renewable for another month at the **Ministry of Immigration**. Once you're there and have established a residence, take proof of your financial solvency, your health insurance policy, and a clearly defined reason for residing in Havana to the Ministry of Immigration (at Calle 22 and Avenida 3 in Miramar).

Student Visas

Most long-term foreign residents I've known were either students at an institution of higher education or invitees doing professional work with a Cuban organization. Visas for these types of travelers are arranged by the organization supporting your travel, which deals directly with the Ministry of Immigration. In fact, if you'd like to actually live in Cuba for an extended period of time, consider registering as a student. The student status opens doors to immigration papers, health insurance, and other benefits of Cuban society.

For information, write to **Mercadu S.A.** at Calle 13, No. 951, esq. Avenida 8, Vedado, Havana 23, C.P. 12300. Or better yet, send them a fax: 33-3028. Check with your nearest Cuban consulate for information on applying to the University of Havana. U.S. citizens should contact the **Cuban Foreign Interests Section** within the Swiss embassy in Washington, D.C. (tel: 202-797-8518; fax: 202-797-8521).

Before planning a long-term study binge, it is recommended that anxiety-prone individuals first visit this very different city to make sure it's the place you'd like to be. The absence of parking lots, Golden Arches, Nike sneakers, multimillion dollar sports stars, and multimillion dollar election campaigns might make you homesick.

Visas for Volunteer Workers

Another "privileged visitor status" is obtained by volunteering. The **U.K. International Work Brigade** (address: 129 Seven Sisters Road, London, N7 7QG; fax: 0171-561-0191), and the **Venceremos Brigade** (address: P.O. Box 7071, Oakland, CA 94601; tel: 510-267-0606) are two established volunteer organizations specializing in Cuba.

Port of Entry

I still had hopes for the bureaucratic nightmare that could earn me a spot on CNN. My next opportunity came when dealing with Cuban immigration officials at Havana's port of entry, the José

Martí International Airport. Maybe I'd resemble a suspected terrorist and be carted off to jail. (Bookselling nowadays requires such publicity.) But each time I enter Havana, not only do immigration agents refuse to give me any hassle, but they don't stamp my passport. As far as the U.S. government is concerned, I've never been to Cuba.

Cuban doctors, teachers, soldiers, and technicians travel around the world helping Third World countries. Cuban immigration agents should join this privileged array of consultants, especially in places like Mexico and Guatemala. (The last time I went to Havana, it was the Mexican immigration official in Cancún who asked for a "tip" in exchange for not stamping my passport, so that there'd be no official evidence that I used Cancún as my exit to Cuba. After talking with hundreds of U.S. citizen travelers to Cuba, I finally found one who was asked by a Cuban immigration agent for a "tip" in exchange for not stamping his passport.)

UTILITIES

Once you've arrived in Havana and a homestay or apartment has found you, what to do about installing utilities? In my research for this chapter, I did a homestay/apartment search throughout the city, and every single available space I could find already had a phone and other utilities. This may change once a real estate industry emerges, but today's custom is to provide you with utilities.

If you happen to find an apartment without a phone, the best strategy is to do as other Cubans do and share the costs of a neighbor's phone. Cubans don't like to do business over the phone, so the telephone is primarily used to say, "I'll meet you at the Hanoi Restaurant at 7 p.m."

A dumb move triggers a weird chain of events. In fact, my only bureaucratic mishap was triggered by my false confidence in the telephone, when I called the "transfer" company to pick me up the next morning to take me to the airport. The cabbie never came. By the time I realized he wouldn't show up, I flagged down a cab on the street, which I should have done in the first place.

This phone-induced mishap expanded into a potentially distressing situation. I arrived at the airport only to learn that they'd changed the schedule of my Cubana de Aviación flight to an hour earlier and the passengers had already boarded. I still had to check in, pay my airport tax, and pass through immigration. I didn't even have time to look at the face of the woman with the sweet voice, probably a Cubana employee, who took me by the arm and rushed me through these steps. They had already closed the gate to the plane when I got there, and I envisioned hiring a *balsero* to row me to Mexico. But then they reopened the gate.

Getting out of Cuba, even for foreigners, seemed more difficult to me than getting in, but that's entirely anecdotal evidence.

TIPS FOR DEALING WITH CUBAN BUREAUCRACIES

1. Faxes, phones and other electronic devices will never replace in-person sessions. Try using a phone to expedite a procedure and it will only cause more delay. Talking out a problem in person, in a friendly way, usually gets the job done. One woman in a town outside of Havana sold me a bus ticket in Cuban pesos when the rules said she couldn't do so, after I explained that I had no other alternatives. Had I phoned her first to save me a trip to the bus station, I'd have gotten nowhere.

   You'd think Cubans would be very rule oriented, given that Cuba is supposed to be a dictatorship, but on various occasions I've had the pleasant experience of Cuban bureaucrats disobeying the letter of the law in order to uphold the spirit of the law. In fact, when doing informal work with Cuban officials, the only bureaucratic snag I was able to encounter was their time-consuming but democratic requirement for consensus for every decision.

2. The performance of Cuban bureaucrats is often measured by statistics. They'll work as hard as necessary if it means accumulating statistics that show their success. Keep this in mind, and find ways in which your business and their performance records merge into a common purpose.

3. More of a universal problem than a Cuban one, I've had experiences in which people at a lower level of a bureaucracy could have given me information they already possessed but were concerned that they were not the official spokesmen for such information, and therefore sent me elsewhere. The elsewheres I went to usually proved fruitful, so I can't complain.

4. Never offer a bribe, even with words like "commission" and "tip." The higher up in the bureaucracy, the less likely there will be any petty corruption. I've seen a few examples of "petite" corruption at the base of the system, as Cuban employees with no dollars struggle to make ends meet. One woman in a museum actually walked out of the museum with me to receive the 10 pesos I was supposed to pay inside for taking a photograph. Whatever Cuban corruption exists at this time can hardly compete with the Mexican or Bolivian varieties I've experienced.

5. Most tasks can get done without any need for dealing with a bureaucrat. The bureaucratic bothers of other countries are simply less likely to occur in Havana, because you the visitor are less likely to own a home, a car or a washing machine. Ownership causes most of the world's bureaucratic problems, and there's so little ownership in Cuba that the likelihood of bureaucratic snags is significantly reduced. When you do need something done, learn to depend on the neighborhood network that you're advised to develop. The neighborhood is Havana's most effectively functioning bureaucratic unit.

Caveat

A few procedural issues not covered here are found within their proper context in other chapters of this book. I apologize for not having presented any Oscar winning bureaucratic nightmares. I did put myself in positions in which they could occur, but somehow I eluded them or they eluded me.

Chapter Eight

MAKING A LIVING
(a.k.a., Generating Income Where Help Is Not Wanted)

No one in his right mind would go to Havana to look for a job. Cubans are usually guaranteed some form of employment, with approximately US$8 to US$25 a month in salary. These jobs are off limits to even the most self-flagellating foreigners who would give up their US$50,000 a year positions to move to Cuba. If Havana's newspapers were to run classified ads sections, they'd have a "help not wanted" section.

It must be understood that, in theory and to a large extent in practice, the low Cuban salaries are compensated for by the fact that many of the daily needs we pay for dearly in our own countries are available to Cuban workers for diminutive and symbolic amounts of money or at no cost at all, including health care, education, culture, part of the monthly food requirements, and athletic facilities.

Basically there are two ways for foreigners to support themselves in Cuba. They may find jobs that are paid for by employers abroad, or they may start a business.

BRING YOUR JOB WITH YOU

Havana must be the only city in the world whose newspapers carry no "help wanted" ads. Visitors who are not in business for themselves must conjure up the most idiosyncratic forms of employment. Some of these "jobs" could involve Cubans as associates, like the visiting photographer who linked up with a Cuban artist to sell post cards to tourists.

To study the possibilities for partnerships with individual Cubans, the potential visitor should ask the nearest Cuban consulate for a copy of the **1993 Ley de Trabajo por Cuenta Propia** (Self-Employment Law) which lists more than 140 modalities of legal self-employment, including food service, taxi driving, bicycle repair, electric repairs, plumbing, shoemaking, and various professional services. At this writing, some 300,000 Cubans are legally self-employed. Since the self-employed are not permitted to "hire" anyone outside of their family (capitalism without exploitation), the foreigner cannot be an employee of the Cuban associate. Legitimately self-employed Cubans must obtain a permit from the government, and monthly tax obligations are rigidly enforced.

Within several sectors of the Cuban economy, such as intercity trains and buses or museums and concerts, foreigners are charged about 20 times the amount that Cubans pay, which rep-

138

resents the difference between the dollar and the Cuban peso. Foreigners do not have access to the subsidized food in Cuban *bodegas*, nor apartments with subsidized rent. This gap in expenses reflects the gap in earning power between Cubans in their peso economy and their foreign counterparts. In plain arithmetic, any economic activity of a self-employed foreign entrepreneur within the Cuban economy would have to be directed towards the tourist market, or the earnings would be insufficient.

That said, foreigners who choose to live the daily life of Cubans to the extent that this is possible will have a very low cost of living and, therefore, any dollars they can earn from abroad will have extraordinary purchasing power. Creating jobs for visitors to Cuba does not fall within the realm of this book, but we can brainstorm with a few examples that may trigger the creativity of readers expecting to arrive in Havana.

1. Cuban music, with its African and jazz rhythms and harmonies blended with components from Spanish tradition, enjoys an extraordinary market abroad. In Japan alone, there are more than 20 salsa bands, and in the United States, musician Ry Cooder compiled a hit recording, *Buena Vista Social Club* (1997), by going to Cuba and performing with veteran *son*, *guajira*, and *danzón* musicians. We do not have to be so enterprising. Armed with a tape recorder, we can apply for a grant from the music department at our local university to record Havana's plethora of sophisticated restaurant and café musicians. (See Chapter 9 on entertainment.) **Tip!** The city of Havana pulsates with music and rhythms at all hours, and a tape recorder helps capture the flavor of the city.

2. In many foreign countries, Havana is perceived as a controversial city, which makes it far more newsworthy than Montevideo in Uruguay or La Paz in Bolivia. Travelers should approach their local newspapers and offer to be their correspondent in Havana for a series of articles on life in the city.

Themes of interest are varied and of cultural and international impact, and can be lifted from within this text.

3. The city's dizzying succession of academic conferences in the arts, medicine, exact sciences, social sciences, religion, agriculture, environment, criminology, popular culture, substance abuse prevention, law, and even yoga, to name but a few, gives anyone in a profession ending with "-ology" a chance to apply for a grant to attend a conference. Marazul Tours in New Jersey will supply you with a list of the year's conferences (fax: 201-319-9009; web site: *http://www.marazutours.com*).

4. Gathering information on health care, education, sports, or other Cuban achievements for your local alternative health care association, school system, or athletic club could net you a travel stipend. Cuba sends teams of doctors, teachers, and athletes as consultants to other countries, so there is considerable demand for such information on an international level.

Note that the above four activities—professional research, freelance journalism, clearly defined educational activities, and information gathering—are listed by the Office of Foreign Assets Control (OFAC) as categories under which United States citizens may apply for and receive a travel license to visit Cuba.

These creative income-generating ideas are just the tip of the iceberg (or, more appropriate for Cuba, the edge of a coral reef) of colorful opportunities for the creative, freelance "hustler." If you know of any company interested in beginning a business in Cuba, why not offer to do some on-the-scene legwork for a salary. (Business research is another category under which OFAC has been granting permission to U.S. citizens to visit Cuba.)

Note: travel restrictions to Cuba only affect U.S. citizens, and by the time you read these pages, they may have been lifted. One indicator that such restrictions will soon become an anachronism is the 1998 initiation of direct flights to Cuba through charter organizations that hire aircraft from major U.S. airlines.

STARTING A BUSINESS

Certain businesses have no future in Havana. Don't even think of opening an athletic club, since Cubans have a wide array of free athletic facilities. Nor should you open a health clinic, because you'll be competing with Cuba's free health care system (it's also prohibited by law). A restaurant may be a good idea, but Mexican or Indian food is out of the question because Cubans don't eat hot, spicy food. Day-care centers, language schools, or technical institutes are out because Havana residents have their education paid for from cradle (literally) to senior citizenship, and education is off limits to foreign investors.

Businesses that do indeed have a great future in Cuba include, first and foremost, the tourist industry, followed by import-export, mining, light industry, and oil exploration (there's oil off the coast but the Cuban government needs financial partners to find it and extract it.) The nation's authorities will especially welcome foreign business people who offer (1) the types of technology that the trade embargo has prevented Cuba from obtaining; (2) a market for Cuban products; (3) fresh capital; and (4) the intangible of social responsibility.

Sharp business people will find other opportunities after visiting Havana and speaking with authorities. It's important to establish contact with Cuban authorities (see Business Directory later in this chapter), for at this moment, most foreign entrepreneurs must establish a partnership with the Cuban government. It also must be understood that Cuba's business laws are constantly changing and that Cuban officials have called the flirtation with foreign capitalists "dancing with the devil." Should they find that foreign business overly disrupts the fundamentals of the Cuban Revolution, they could conceivably devise a more rigid set of laws.

The good news is that the type of rampant corruption that poisons relationships with most Latin American governments and

141

foreign capitalists is virtually nonexistent in Cuba, according to John Kavulich, president of the U.S.-Cuba Trade and Economic Council (web site listed later in this chapter).

Joint Ventures

In 1992 only 50 joint enterprises existed between foreigners and the Cuban government, representing only 10 countries. By 1996, however, more than 200 joint enterprises involved in 34 branches of the economy were representing 55 countries. Cuba is one of the world's last frontiers for international business investment, but if you don't get in soon, the best opportunities may have already been taken. Potential foreign investors should know that Cuba's labor force is highly qualified, with an average of between 10 and 11 years of schooling, and with a culture that places great esteem in learning.

Under Cuba's **Ley de Inversión Extranjera** (Foreign Investment Law), foreign companies do not become sole owners of property. The Cuban type of joint enterprise means that both parties, foreign investor and Cuban government, share the property as well as the administration of the business. Profits from any business are divided equally between the two partners, with the half going to the foreign entrepreneur taxed at a reasonable rate.

The **1996 Helms-Burton Act** allows U.S. business interests to take legal action in U.S. courts against any foreign company that utilizes property in Cuba confiscated in the Revolution. However, at this writing, Helms-Burton has been so unpopular throughout the world, that de facto noncompliance reigns, except, of course, within the United States. Even the two nearest trading partners with the United States, Canada and Mexico, have openly defied Helms-Burton.

At the same time, even with the trade embargo still in force, the United States Department of Commerce has been granting permission to U.S. corporations to explore the business market in

Cuba. Many United States business leaders, upset that their competition has had the upper hand in what was traditionally the U.S. sphere of influence, were elated when the Pope condemned the embargo during his January 1998 visit to Cuba.

One quirk in the Cuban business scene is that the Cuban government determines the salaries of workers in foreign firms, in a desperate attempt to maintain social equality. Nevertheless, at least within the tourist industry, tips earned by Cuban workers put them in an advantageous position.

Many Canadian business people seem to relish helping Cuba's economy recover from the near catastrophe of the Special Period. "Canada has become a catalyst for Cuba's economic rehabilitation," according to a 1997 *Maclean's* article. Anyone who has seen the sparkling new, modernist José Martí International Airport or some of the seminal inner city rehabilitation projects (all of the above financed with Canadian money) comes away with the impression that Canada has taken a passionate interest in disrupting the U.S. economic embargo.

Rules

Rules for setting up a business will be listed here, but as mentioned before, Cuba's business scene is changing on a yearly, monthly, and sometimes daily basis. "Anything that's prohibited today may be allowed tomorrow," says John Kavulich, "and anything allowed today might be prohibited tomorrow." For this reason, the first step for any foreigner interested in doing business in and with Cuba is an appointment with a business specialist at the nearest Cuban consulate.

A Cuban business official, interviewed in Havana by this writer, supplied us with the basic requirements for starting up a business in Cuba. In reference to the **1995 Ley 77, La Inversión Extranjera** (Law 77, Foreign Investment), any sector except for the armed forces, education, and public health is open to foreign

143

investors, with limitations placed on retail businesses. By far the most common modality is the *empresa mixta* (joint enterprise) between a foreign entrepreneur and the Cuban government. (The exceptions that permit 100 percent foreign investment concern sectors of the economy that are strategically vital to Cuba.) Associations have been created within Cuba to deal with real estate, industrial parks, and duty-free zones.

The foreigner would do best to fulfill three major roles: (1) contribute capital; (2) contribute technology; and (3) supply a market for the Cuban product.

"These are considered prerequisites," said the official, "but in some cases, exceptions have been made when the foreign investor complies with two of the three requirements." For information and negotiation on business proposals, the most important site in Havana is the **Ministerio de Inversión Extranjera** (Ministry of Foreign Investment), located in the Playa district (Miramar), 1st Avenue and 18th Street. An easier option, according to the official, is to seek out an executive from a state enterprise, and have that Cuban enterprise do the paperwork.

The Cuban Exception

It is absolutely prohibited for Cuban officials to receive a "commission" from foreign business applicants. For those of us who have lived in other Latin American countries, such an affirmation is nothing short of bizarre. Yet the certitude of the virtually corruption-free Cuban business scene was emphasized after the Cuban official I had interviewed had departed; his friends told me that the he lived a very frugal life.

"He has many tribulations," they said, "all based on his economic limitations."

That he refrains from accepting bribes represents "the Cuban exception" in reference to the rest of Latin America. Two contradictory factors prevent someone like this gentleman from engaging in corruption: (1) a belief in the ideals of the Cuban Revolution and (2) the fear of legal penalties if he were caught. Whether you agree or not with the ideological foundation of the Cuban Revolution, rest assured that if unbridled capitalism and a typical Latin American plutocracy ever replaced the current Cuban system, a notable escalation in corruption would follow. For the time being, though, Cuba continues to grope for a happy ground between capitalist development and socialist benefits.

"Whatever may happen," said one high-ranking Cuban official to this writer, "we will never give ground on our free education and health systems."

Business Directory
All Havana phone/fax numbers should be preceded by the prefix 53-7 (the country and city codes).

- A primary source for business updates on Cuba is the **U.S.-Cuba Trade and Economic Council** a nonpolitical organization headed by John Kavulich and based in New York (web site: *http://www.cubatrade.org*). This organization has been responsible for helping U.S. investors and entrepreneurs to get OFAC licenses to travel to Cuba.
- **CONAVANA, S.A.** (Consultores de Avalúos Naciones) is a group of Cuban business consultants specializing in foreign business start-ups, property appraisal, feasibility studies, and engineering advice. Located at Calle 8 No. 306 between 13th and 15th Streets in Vedado, Havana (tel: 33-7342; fax: 33-7341; e-mail: *conavana@colombus.cu*).
- **Centro de Promoción de Inversiones, MINVEC**, is a government intermediary that arranges partnerships with foreign entrepreneurs. Located at Avenida 1ra, no. 1404, between 14th and 16th Streets in Miramar, Havana (fax: 32-2105).
- **Bolsa de Subcontratación** (Subcontracting Exchange) is a resource center for the latest industrial opportunities. Located

145

at Edificio FOCSA, 1er piso, Apt. 1B, between 17th Street and North Vedado, Havana (tel: 30-9556; fax: 32-2105).

- **CEPEC** is the Cuban government export department. Located at Infanta #16, Vedado, Havana. (tel: 74-2185; fax: 78-6234).
- **Consultoría Jurídica Internacional** (International Legal Office) helps guide foreign clients through bureaucratic procedures related to setting up a business, including contracts, joint-enterprise documents, brand-name and patent registration, notary services, immigration papers, and powers-of-attorney. Staffed by attorneys, economists, and insurance specialists. Located at Calle 18 #120, corner of Avenida 3ra, Miramar, Playa, Havana (fax: 33-2303).

Getting Started

The first step in the process is to consult with the business attaché of your nearest Cuban consulate. Procedures may change, and before spinning an impossible web of contacts, get advice on the most updated strategy from the Cuban consulate. If you're in Havana for business purposes, notice that most of the agencies and ministries you may have to visit are located either in Vedado or Miramar, so a hotel in Old Havana, although aesthetically pleasing, will add to your taxi mileage and eat up your working time.

THE ECONOMIC EMBARGO

The U.S. economic embargo, unpopular throughout the world and supported by just two countries in the United Nations (one of which, Israel, now does business with Cuba), seems to hang on out of habit. The Soviets are no longer in Cuba, free enterprise (with controls), is permitted, and Cuba's human rights record is better than that of many countries who enjoy the "most-favored-nation" trading status with the United States.

Hopefully, by the time this book is in print, you'll be able to rip out these pages, but with the intransigence of the U.S. foreign policy, the embargo might well be with us for a few more years. If this is the case, let us examine how the embargo affects potential business investment in Cuba.

First and foremost, business people from countries with less pull than the U.S. still have a chance to get a jump on United States corporations. However, there has been all kinds of movement from within the United States, independent of Congress and the Cuban exile lobby. Through the U.S.-Cuba Trade and Economic Council, U.S. business people have been assisted in getting permission from OFAC to travel to Cuba in order to research trade in medical equipment/supplies and pharmaceuticals.

Nonpolitical, international humanitarian organizations labeled the embargo an affront to human rights, particularly in the realm of health care products, some of which are totally controlled by U.S. corporations and their foreign subsidiaries. Innocent Cuban civilians suffer the consequences. Even if the embargo is maintained, the most likely "reform" would be a lifting of the prohibition for selling medical supplies to Cuba. Cuba's X-ray machines need spare parts that are only manufactured by U.S. companies. A decade ago, the Cubans had a choice of replacing all their X-ray equipment with Japanese products, but given their historical affinities with the United States, right or wrong, they chose to hold on until the embargo was lifted. A recent OFAC license was granted to U.S. medical supply companies to organize a trade fair in Cuba.

Loophole business openings with Cuba go beyond market research for medical products. OFAC licenses for "familiarization tours" to Cuba have been granted to senior-level executives of U.S. airlines, hotel operators, vehicle rental companies, and financial service companies, with these visits fully hosted by Cuba's largest tourism company, Havanatur. Representatives from the U.S. music industry also visited Cuba, with OFAC licenses, to explore the possibilities of imports and exports. Cuban music is a

147

hot commodity in Europe and parts of Asia, and many citizens from the United States go out of their way to purchase their Cuban music through third countries.

Whether you like him or not, Fidel Castro is a unique symbol for many Latin American intellectuals, economists, and students—he's a national leader who has stood up to the United States. At the 1993 inauguration of a new Bolivian president, Fidel received a much heartier and sustained round of applause than the president-elect, who later remarked, "It seems like Fidel Castro, and not me, has won the election."

The dominant theory of respected analysts for the persistence of the embargo is that the United States does not want any economic success in Cuba that could inspire other Latin countries to seek a path independent of U.S. economic hegemony. The supporters of the embargo may be holding out until Fidel Castro, the symbol, passes away. But Cuban authorities laugh at typical questions like "what will happen after Fidel?" since they believe their revolutionary "process" will continue.

Ever since Benjamin Franklin, John Adams, and Thomas Jefferson declared their interest in annexing Cuba, this little island has sent big waves crashing upon U.S. shores.

— Chapter Nine —

STREET-LIFE AND ENTERTAINMENT

Take the most misanthropic, sour souls in the world, the most negative thinkers we know, and put them on a plane to Havana. Choose those acquaintances who simply do not know how to have a good time. Drop them off on a street in Havana, give them the key to a room at a homestay, and leave them on their own.

It is said that one negative thinker in a room of a hundred optimists can bring down the optimists and cloud their horizons. But the gloomy soul we drop off in Havana has little or no chance to sustain his murky outlook in this town. He'll be dealing with people who, even during the most penurious years of the Special Period (1991 to 1996), when facing a dramatic food crisis, regular power blackouts, drastic shortages in pharmaceutical products, and two-hour waits for buses which had run out of fuel, maintained their *joie de vivre*.

"You would think that this type of life would make the people on our street become choleric and irritable," stated a *Newsweek* article written during the period of crisis in Havana. "But even when Havana presents an aspect similar to cities affected by wars, its inhabitants do not appear to be suffering. And most important, they are not even under much pressure, and if anything they are carefree."

Now, at the turn of the century, blackouts are rare, economical farmers' markets are springing up everywhere, buses run more regularly, and the Cuban medical establishment has conjured up "green medicine" substitutes for those pharmaceutical products not produced in Cuba and subject to the embargo. Although life remains tough, the *joie de vivre* of Havana residents remains resilient, and Habaneros even find ways to convert their griping into a humorous art form. Even during the intense core of the economic crisis, idealistic city planners were busy restoring the city's colonial center brick by brick, and salsa musicians were coming up with the some of the most daring rhythmic and harmonic innovations in the history of music.

Our sour friends whom we dropped off on the streets of Havana will not have to search for entertainment venues, theater tickets, or special events in order to wipe away their gloom. In Havana, entertainment is primarily the street itself, the park, the Malecón, the corner bar, the plaza, the beach, and the people who frequent these places.

A superficial analysis will conclude that *joie de vivre* is determined by cultural heritage and that some peoples are more joy-loving than others. Another observation simply too obvious to be taken seriously is that the climate of a place somehow determines whether people are outgoing (like Cubans) or introspective, as people from cold climates are supposed to be. Like many stereotypes, there is probably a partial truth to these assumptions. But I have been in tropical Latin American cities which were gloomy, depressing places. On the other hand, even during the cold, misty Paris winter when outdoor chairs are moved to the inside of cafes, the *joie de vivre* of Parisian cafe culture persists.

SENSE OF PLACE

The entertainment of Havana's street-life has much to do with the city's very unique sense of place, and that the physical layout, in particular the wealth of public gathering place, greatly contributes to its sense of joy.

In *The Great Good Place*, urbanologist Ray Oldenburg observes, "Great civilizations, like great cities share a common feature. Evolving within them and crucial to their growth and refinement are distinctive public gathering places. These become as much a part of the urban landscape as of the citizen's daily life and, invariably, they come to dominate the image of the city."

Oldenburg calls these public gathering places Great Good Places, where "the stranger feels at home . . . In cities without them, even the native does not feel at home. Without such places, the urban area fails to nourish the kinds of relationships and the diversity of human contact that are the essence of the city."

Havana is blessed with this public realm, but I've seen other cities with just as much public space, with much of it empty. Havana not only has its public gathering spaces, but knows how to fill them. The contrast is the emptiness of so many streets and public parks in the U.S.A., for example, because citizens go to their private garage, get into their private car, and drive through empty streets without stores or street vendors to immense parking lots where they engage in the commerce that was not available in their neighborhood.

Traditionally, neighborhoods contained not only residences but grocery stores, doctors, cafés, beauty parlors, workshops, religious centers, and offices. Under modern single-use zoning codes, commerce has been rigidly isolated from residence. "As a result,"

151

according to an *American Enterprise* article, "the elements a household needs in a typical day are diffused over a wide area."

"The traditional pattern of walkable, mixed-use neighborhoods has been prohibited," adds architect Andres Duany. Could it be that Havana's mixed-use, walkable streets encourage the *joie de vivre* of its inhabitants while the single-use zoning of many North American cities does the opposite? If this were true, then cliches about cultural and climate differences would be secondary to the structure of a city in determining the level of informal and serendipitous interaction among its inhabitants.

In *The Geography of Nowhere*, James Howard Kunstler attributes the lack of public human interaction in the United States to a type of automobile determinism that takes people off the streets. He echoes the sentiments of Duany, that the predominance of single-use zoning, which separates commerce from residence and obligates people to hop into a car to do their errands, has created a man-made wasteland.

"Since World War II," he writes, "we have managed to turn America into a nation of places that are hardly worth caring about. Few localities have managed to escape the plague of strip-mall banality, mutilation by freeway, chain store pillage, single-use zoning idiocy, and other mechanisms of degradation."

Kunstler cannot emphasize enough the role of the automobile in impoverishing the urban environment. "We've turned American towns and cities into auto storage depots that only incidentally contain other things. By subordinating so many other aspects of our lives to the car, we have created places unworthy of affection."

Havana offers a striking contrast to the images of urban and suburban United States presented by Kunstler and Oldenburg. There are no ugly parking structures or blighting parking lots because few Habaneros own their own automobiles. Commerce is within walking distance of residence and even districts known to be "commercial" contain apartment buildings. One walks out the front door and comes into immediate contact with humanity, casual friends, personalized commercial services, children playing stickball in the street (since few cars are likely to pass), neighborhood "characters" who are the idiosyncratic pillars of the community, and even one's family physician, who never lives more than a block or two away.

He's called "Colorado." He hangs out every day on the Prado, helping people find whatever they need. "I'm smoking the best cigar in the world," he says.

153

Classic cars are a part of the Havana cityscape.

When you do bump into parked cars, they are usually collectors items — Fords, Chevys, and Plymouths from the 1940s, '50s, and early '60s. Even the automobile landscape of the city bears closer resemblance to an outdoor museum than to a consumer, throwaway society.

What you are most likely to find in Havana are what Oldenburg labels "Third Places." The first place is one's home and the second place is work. Too many people in the U.S., according to Oldenburg, shuffle back between first and second places with no third place for unwinding from their daily routine. "Daily life in the new urban sprawl," he writes, "is like a grammar school with no recess periods."

In Havana, life's recess periods, which take place in an astounding number and variety of "third places," is the major form of the city's entertainment. You don't drive 30 miles to a venue of entertainment. It's right there around the corner. Havana is one long extended recess period!

154

Such constant interaction with casual friends, neighbors, and strangers can seem too intense for those who come from cultures that revere privacy. Oldenburg fears such a disappearance of community in his country.

"America does not rank well on the dimension of her informal public life and less well now than in the past," he writes. "Increasingly, her citizens are encouraged to find their relaxation, entertainment, companionship, even safety, almost entirely within the privacy of homes that have become more a retreat from society than a connection to it."

Consider Oldenburg's statement in relationship to the structure of Havana. The back deck and back yard, affording privacy for millions of U.S. citizens, are a rare occurrence in the Havana landscape. Instead, there are the front balconies that connect residence with street, neighbors with neighbors. Instead of the private backyard, there are community gardens.

As with middle- and working-class residents of Manhattan or Paris, Habaneros live in cramped quarters by suburban North American standards, with the trade-off being ready access to free culture, athletic facilities, health care, and above all an extended outdoor living room that belongs to the whole neighborhood.

Streets for the Masses

The stationary bicycle that allows Americans to do exercise privately (although most stationary bicycles end up as abandoned artifacts, instruments of intolerable tedium) is contrasted by Havana's outdoor bicycle culture. In their *Healthy Pleasures*, doctors Robert Ornstein and David Sobel refer to a North American by the name of George and his "Exercist bicycle."

"George spends almost his entire day abstaining from any meaningful physical activity. Then, four times a week, he faithfully follows his prescription of thirty-plus minutes of aerobic exercise at 70 percent of maximum intensity four times a week."

155

Insisting on the concept of "purposeful exercise," the authors suggest, "Instead of following his exercise prescription, George might have bicycled or walked to work..."

At the onset of the 1990s, Fidel Castro asserted (in declaring Cuba's new "era of the bicycle") that the fuel crisis was a blessing in disguise that would improve the health of Cubans who chose to cycle to work instead of taking the bus. I know of one former Havana resident who, disregarding the advice of both the good doctors and Fidel, became a bicycle refugee and went to California, where he now commutes to work in his private automobile.

Havana residents either walk or bicycle to their favorite Third Places. They have plenty of time for leisure since the number of hours in the work week for many Habaneros has been cut so that everyone can have a job. One of my friends, a hyperproductive scientist, works every other day. An article in a U.S. newspaper referred to a recent Cuban immigrant who found that Americans work too hard. The absence of Third Places in the urban landscape of many U.S. cities may be in part related to the work ethic. How can you hang out in a cafe for hours and hours when there are things to do?

"But our health, happiness, and future," according to Ornstein and Sobel, "depend upon understanding and reversing this deep-rooted cultural denial of pleasure and leisure."

Another advantage of public gathering places is that they offer free entertainment, or hours of lively conversation for the cost of a beer or a cup of coffee. Entertainment is not something that is watched but, rather, participated in. The people in one's neighborhood are the de facto entertainers. As it is, Havana's more formal venues of entertainment (except tourist traps), are remarkably inexpensive. Culture and sports were considered a right and not a privilege by those who molded Cuba after 1959, and admission to concerts, dance gatherings, and athletic events is either free or at a nominal cost.

156

Can Habaneros be happy without their own cars, backyards, elaborate home entertainment centers, private swimming pools, or walk-in closets? According to indexes which measure happiness, increases in wealth do indeed bring increases in happiness for people who were living below the poverty line. But once a person achieves a minimal standard of living, "increases in wealth don't seem to matter so much," according to Ornstein and Sobel.

There exists the "cage of gold" syndrome in which some people's happiness actually decreases with additions to their private wealth. An elaborate home entertainment center can keep a person so busy with himself that he becomes estranged from society and suffers the symptoms of loneliness.

For years I lived in Maryland and southern California. On countless occasions, I walked by the houses of neighbors, with the cars of people who arrived from 30 miles away parked our front. Never did I expect to be invited to their get-togethers, and I never was. Neighbors had little contact, since they rarely used the sidewalk in front of their houses, instead leaving home only by way of their garage. On numerous occasions in Havana, how-

157

ever, I was walking down the street (and approaching the sounds of rumba) when from open front doors or balconies, random strangers or people who had seen me in the neighborhood motioned for me to come in and join the fun. The barrier between residence and street hardly existed.

With few cars passing by, the street belongs to the neighbors who live there. The street is the first and foremost public gathering place for it is right outside one's apartment. This reminds me of certain old neighborhoods in New York in which, even today, people sit and chat on stoops in front of their apartments as their children play in the street.

Havana's landscape of public gathering places is described in the neighborhood tour in Chapter 1. The best strategy for participating in the city's public life is to establish yourself in a neighborhood, spend as much time as possible within a small radius of your apartment, and remain as far away as possible from any hotel. As a foreigner, you may be seen at first by street hustlers as their opportunity to make a few dollars. But once you become

Fishing off the Malecón with the El Morro fortress in the background.

known as a regular, they'll salute and chat without trying to sell you anything.

Popular games in parks, bars, and on strolling lanes include dominoes and chess, although the art of conversation is still the number one form of entertainment. You'll automatically be part of a subcultural community should you decide to go fishing or swimming near the wall of La Punta (the Point) on the Malecón. Patronizing your local sandwich or coffee vendor on a regular basis will bring you into contact with groups that hang out on curbsides in front of these establishments. You won't remain lonely in the crowd because Habaneros will be curious to find out about you.

The History Factor

Havana's urban sense of place is partly determined by history, although it is difficult to explain why a historical setting contributes to the positive interaction of neighbors. Sociologist David Reisman studied the disastrous consequences of North American "urban renewal" and New Town projects that knocked down existing neighborhoods and replaced them with more modern ones. Reisman concluded that "there were values concealed in the most seemingly depressed urban conglomerations which were lost in the move to more hygienic and aseptic planned communities."

One notes the different feel of different Havana neighborhoods; the more modern streets of Cerro, for example, don't quite measure up to the older, battered streets of Centro Habana when it comes human interaction. I had the same impression, although more fleeting, when comparing the older but ungentrified neighborhoods of Quebec to the more impersonal higher part of the city beyond the city center.

Nowhere is the inhumanity of urban renewal more evident than in Detroit. In his essay "Defining a Sense of Place," Pierce Lewis wrote: "The Detroit planners of the 1950s made the assumption that old things were bad things and eagerly tore down

almost everything that dated from the nineteenth century . . .
People who opposed those views were dismissed as reactionary,
and a good share of the city was destroyed . . . As the old houses
were torn down, the people fled, and as the old monuments were
leveled, there was less and less reason for native Detroiters to
return to the city of their birth." (It's no coincidence that when
the directors of the film *Robocop* sought an ideal setting to capture
a cruel, modernist civilization, they chose downtown Detroit.)

It is worth repeating here that the Havana restoration brigade, under the prophetic guidance of Eusebio Leal, is thanking
the lucky stars that during the modernist international building
boom of the second half of the twentieth century, Havana was
literally abandoned by the state and private property speculation
was prohibited by the socialist government. These pioneers in
restoration are also keenly aware that historical setting plays a
vital role in a sense of community, and therefore fight to preserve
the residential facets of Old Havana and Centro Habana. They
are aware of the failed "Old Towne" projects which left places
like Williamsburg or Old Town Sacramento divorced from ev-
eryday life—so-called "fake places" that "compared to the river of
time . . . are like bottled water: harmless, perhaps useful, but not
very nourishing," as Pierce Lewis eloquently notes. He adds: "We
have treated history as an item, which can be fenced off from the
'real world.'" Havana restoration projects are dedicated to keeping the real world within their boundaries, and thus far, even with
the rapidly expanding presence of tourists, community gathering
places thrive in the historical setting of Old Havana.

Whether these visionaries of restoration can stave off
gentrification depends on the nature of transitions in Cuba in the
next decade. A free-market real estate economy could turn Old
Havana into something similar to the Marais district of Paris, a
perfect and stunning specimen of restored history whose high rents
make it off-limits to working class Parisians.

The Density Factor

I grew up in a dense place in New York with a low crime rate. I was led to believe that high population density was a bad thing because people had no room to move about and did not enjoy the tranquilizing effects of nature. Today I'd love to bring charges against the people who subjected me to such mental violence and fine them for the billions of dollars in losses of community.

Memphis, Tennessee developer Henry M. Turley, Jr. recognizes the mistakes of the anti-density ideology of city planners.

"I build developments dense enough to allow walking and freedom from cars—developments with sidewalks and places to which they can take us: stores, schools, and a town hall right in the community, not down the highway."

People in this dense Old Havana neighborhood find everything they need within easy walking or cycling distance.

161

Cuban democracy, whatever its well-publicized shortcomings at the national level, is based on the town meeting, and every neighborhood elects its own representatives. Neighbors participate in forums within walking distance of their apartments, and the relative critical silence of the written press in Cuba is contrasted by the critical outspokenness of the neighbors in their forums. Habaneros don't depend on TV for their political activity. It is right around the corner . . .

As is the family doctor, who lives within the same neighborhood quadrant where he practices his profession. Density allows for community cohesion.

One of the fears instilled upon us about population density is the element of crime. We were led to believe that somehow, density of living arrangements correlated directly with the amount of crime in a neighborhood. I had no idea at the time that population density in South Central Los Angeles and other riot torn neighborhoods was considerably less than in safe neighborhoods like nearby Santa Monica.

The Safety Factor

Had I not been questioned on a regular basis about Havana's safety, it never would have occurred to me to deal with the subject. But the knee-jerk question of people from other countries concerns how safe it is to hang out on Havana's urban streets, especially late at night.

According to the *Newsweek* article previously cited, "People with experience say that the worse that can happen to you on any street in Havana is that you'll be pickpocketed or tricked out of your money. Violent crimes are extremely rare."

The fact that people actually know each other in a neighborhood is a form of social protection. But rising crime (by Cuban standards) during the economic crisis of the Special Period, especially in and around tourist hotels, prompted the government to add police to every corner, partially analogous to the crime-prevention measures taken by Mayor Giuliani during the same period in New York City.

Typical of Cuba's prevailing social philosophy, when there is a conflict between public and private rights, public rights prevail. Never a dangerous city, an increase in crime prompted Cuban officials to crack down. That meant stopping people on occasion for no reason but to ask for their I.D. Cubans talking with tourists were prime targets. That's the bad news, and some enraged Habaneros are making their disagreements known at neighborhood forums, and in direct dialogue with the police.

The good news is that Havana's ubiquitous "Officer Friendly" is unarmed, as are Havana's criminals, and bribery or extortion by the police (a regular occurrence in most Latin American cities) is foreign to Havana. Without suggesting you count your dollars in public or wear shiny jewelry while on the street, hanging out in any of Havana's outdoor or indoor public gathering places is comparatively safer than doing the same in other major cities of the world, where a lack of urban intimacy allows potential muggers the freedom of anonymity.

What could be dangerous is accepting invitations to the homes of strangers. For most other countries this would not even be an issue, but in Havana one is constantly being invited into people's homes. Habaneros want to sell us cigars or cassettes, introduce us to their mothers, or simply invite us to a cup of Cuban coffee. Some of my Havana friends have warned me to be careful about entering apartments, probably rightfully so since there's no police protection in a dark, labyrinthine corridor of an ancient Havana tenement.

But dutifully I've entered whenever invited and unfortunately suffered none of the type of misadventures that could have helped me sell books.

163

THE ALTERNATIVE TROPICANA

You must visit the **Tropicana**, located at Calle 72, No 4504, in Marianao (tel: 33-7507). That's what all the tourist pamphlets advise. It only costs about US$40 to get in, and after that, a mere bottle of Cuban rum won't run you more than US$50 or US$60. After all the extras are included, you can probably get out of there minus only US$200, the yearly salary of most Cubans.

In my neighborhood, there's another outdoor cabaret, with no obvious name. By day it looks like a cement platform sur-rounded by a few vending stalls, with tropical trees providing background shade. It's open Friday and Saturday nights and you can't miss it. It's at the end of El Prado, on the corner of Genio, just before you get to the park across from La Punta. Admission is US$1. Beer is a buck and a *mojito* is US$2.50. So how does this compare with the Tropicana?

The house band is called Grupo Artístico Onareo Adolfo Guzmán, and its list of musicians is twice as long as the name of the group. The band dresses in bright red jackets, the color of Changó, the Yoruban equivalent of Santa Barbara and the *orisha* of fire, thunder, drums, and virility—an inspiration for Afro-Cu-ban rhythms. There are three singers: a blond woman with lots of makeup who seems like a leftover from the Batista days, a slick crooner who was once a ladies' man, and an attractive young Afro-Cuban woman with a silky voice that covers several octaves and gets deep and emotional at just the right time. The dancers, dressed in various rococo styles, are not the perfect specimens you'd find at the Tropicana, but they can move with the best of them. The male dancers are sleek and agile. There are lots of legs and flesh waved around by the brigade of female dancers.

Few Cubans can afford the Tropicana, of course, and those who can, well, you wonder where they get their money. The Tropicana is essentially for tourists. So, you've seen something Cuban, but not with Cubans. On the other hand, at the unnamed club I stumbled upon one Friday night, there were mainly Cubans in the audience. In fact, some of the Cubans were there to party with their children.

For Habaneros who couldn't afford the dollar admission, there was a place just outside the transparent wire fence that surrounded the club. For them it was like watching a baseball game from behind the net that drapes behind home plate. There was a festive atmosphere both inside and outside the linked fence. Some of the neighbors in the empty lot outside had brought their own beer and were munching on toasted peanuts.

I had run into this place while walking home. The animator outside the entrance gate grabbed me by the arm.

"Give us a try," he said. "You'll love the dancers. In fact, I'll let you in for free. Just promise me that if you enjoy the show, you'll bring some friends tomorrow night."

I offered him a dollar, which he refused to take as he escorted me in. Within a few minutes, he'd brought me a shot of rum. "On the house," he said.

I still can't figure why he'd been so generous, since the place was packed and they didn't need more people. Perhaps, I thought, it was because I was a new face and the other people were regulars. After the first few songs and dances, a traditional Cuban *son*, some salsa, and a Brazilian samba, my host came over and took me took me to another table, where he introduced me to his wife and three children. His wife invited me to have another rum.

The next night, as promised, I invited two Cuban friends, Tomás and Caridad. I asked them how this show compared, by Cuban standards, to the Tropicana.

"Very well," said Tomás. "I haven't been to the Tropicana, but I can assure you these are true professionals."

I could tell Caridad enjoyed the music because she was singing along with the chorus and ready to burst out of her seat to dance.

Lead singer with Grupo Artístico Onareo Adolfo Guzmán.

Dancers with Grupo Artístico Onareo Adolfo Guzmán.

The people outside the fence were hopping and clapping. And from across the street, neighbors leaning out of second floor baroque balconies were enjoying the best seats in, and outside, the house. The band played virtually every Cuban genre of music, but in particular, their rendition of traditional *sones* was memorable. I know because I was humming those tunes in the shower for the next several days.

I have nothing against the Tropicana. It's a superb nightclub. But the unnamed Tropicana-style outdoor club in my neighborhood was much more than a nightclub. It was what Ray Oldenburg would call a Great Good Place. It didn't have the 200 dancers who appear at the Tropicana, but how many dancers do you need to see in one evening?

The best way to find these places is simply to stroll through the streets. They are everywhere. The alternative Tropicana only opens at night, but music can be heard and then found at all hours in most central neighborhoods.

The idea of entertainment as a break from daily life, a separate place we visit and then depart from, does not fit the city of Havana. Here, entertainment and daily life are inseparable. The public gathering place, whether it be an ornate, tree-covered center strip of a boulevard with stone-sculpted benches (El Prado), the seawall across the north end of the city (El Malecón), animated parks, neighborhood taverns, streetside snack stands, public plazas with outdoor cafes and book vendors, or the street itself, is Havana's daily entertainment, with friends, neighbors, and strangers, as well as the protagonists.

MUSEUMS FOR PEOPLE
WHO DON'T LIKE MUSEUMS

Funny thing happened on the way to the museum. I got swept away by a rumba party. Next day I got distracted by the sea breeze and went to the beach. With so much happening in Havana's public places, it's not easy to elude the action and duck into a museum. But this city's museums, especially the quirkier ones, will be a refreshing surprise for visitors who hate museums.

It's not like the Louvre, where you get lost in a place whose square footage covers as much territory as a small city. Many of Havana's museums remain on an intimate and human scale. The contents are often surprising, but even when the exhibits don't transcend the typical museum fare, the setting is dazzling. When visiting Havana museums, you become a peeping tom into colonial interiors that were off-limits to the public in their times. Floors with colorful marble or mosaic designs, ornate wrought-iron balconies on winding staircases, rococo wall moldings, interior patios surrounded by arcade balconies with Doric pillars and Gothic vaults, high windows and higher ceilings that dissipate the claustrophobia usually associated with museums.

Like Havana's mixed-use neighborhoods, many of her museums lack the single-use unity of a perfect and boring museum. There's the juxtaposing of elements that are not supposed to come together. Some exhibits lack the necessary written explanations to make sense, so you hire a guide for an extra two dollars, or better yet, bring a Habanero friend who identifies with what's inside.

I got Soledad, whose mother is a believer in Santería, to accompany me to the **Museo Municipal de Regla**. As expected, the collections were eclectic, relating to Regla's participation in independence struggles, her archeological past, and her Afro-Cuban heritage, much alive today. Most impressive are the artifacts and clothing related to Santería. What could have been a bunch of attractive but stray and forgettable items, came alive with Soledad's reexperiencing of her childhood religious upbringing. And by being here I discovered why I was here. It was Eleggua, lord of the crossroads, guardian of our destiny, dressed in my favorite anarchist colors, red and black, who is there to guide our way.

Schoolchildren visiting the Municipal Museum of Regla.

I decided to leave my fate in the hands of Elegguá, who guided us past a *santera* woman smoking a cigar, back to the ferry, and into the streets of Old Havana. With no plan in mind, no guidebook in hand, we were told by Elegguá to enter into the shadowy arches of an attractive colonnade and into a colonial building over checkerboard mosaic floor tiles. We were led to the headquarters of Eusebio Leal Spengler, the mastermind of Havana's restoration. This was the **Museo de la Ciudad**, and by now you've concluded that *museo* means "museum."

Here, I found artwork, historical exhibits, ethnology, archeology, folklore, and the usual armaments from the era of non-televised wars. On the second floor, overlooking an interior garden, were finely-worked, sparkling, white stone facades that appeared to have been sandblasted only yesterday. I looked for Mr. Leal and by a twist of fate he was not there. I'd come from Bolivia to find him, but he had traveled to Bolivia probably to give a lecture.

170

Instead I talked with his secretary, a friendly and distinguished woman who spoke with the diplomacy of an ambassador and the enthusiasm of a crusader. Upon discovering my interest in Havana's restoration, she presented me with a superb book of photos and elaborate maps of restoration plans, *Viaje en la memoria* (A Voyage in Memory). I applauded her good fortune to be working in an office whose newest furniture dated back to 1789.

I didn't need Elegguá to lead me to El Morro, whose full name is **Parque Histórico Militar Morro-Cabaña**, a museum without being called *museo*. To not see this fortress across the bay from the Malecón would be equivalent to not seeing the Eiffel Tower in Paris. And in fact, the same French lighting system used at night in the Eiffel Tower is now used at this Havana fortress-lighthouse. Eiffelization is France's answer to Disnification.

171

You can reach El Morro by *cyclobus* from the park across from La Punta. Within this massive fortress, which was built to protect Havana from pirate attacks, you get pretty much what you expect: a history of armaments and military architecture, and detailed exhibits related to navigation and the defense of the city. Machinery buffs will be pleased to examine centuries-old wooden machinery. What doesn't belong here may be the museum's most attractive feature: a colorful exhibition of art naif paintings hung on ancient walls in a structure whose interior resembles renaissance Florence.

Entrance to Havana museums is usually US$2 plus an added cost for picture-taking. Cubans pay one or two pesos. Most museums are open all week between 9:00 a.m. and 9:00 p.m., but some are closed on Mondays.

Museum Menu

The best of the rest of Havana's other great museums are listed below. (All are located in Old Havana except the Museo Histórico de Guanabacoa, which is across the bay in Guanabacoa.)

- The **Museo Casa Natal de José Martí** is worth visiting if for no other reason that Martí is one of the most visionary figures in modern history and Cuba's most revered national hero. You get little of the feel of antiquity inside, but a few inspiring quotes from Martí could alter the course of your life.
- The **Museo de la Revolución y Memorial Granma** is for Cuban Revolution fans. Check out the Da Vinci-like ceiling mural.
- **Casa de Africa** has items from 26 countries in Africa, including gifts from African personalities to Fidel Castro. There's an emphasis on those objects used in Afro-Cuban religions.
- The **Museo Histórico de Guanabacoa**, located in the heart of a district where Afro-Cuban religions prevail, offers more exhibits on Santerían heritage. Enjoy an attractive colonial patio and interiors that date back as far as the 16th century.

STREET-LIFE AND ENTERTAINMENT

- The **Museo de Arte Colonial** (right across from the Cathedral in Old Havana), is, both outside and inside, a remarkable trip back through the centuries.
- The **Museo Nacional de la Música** is for lovers of both Cuban and European classical music.
- The **Museo Nacional de Bellas Artes** has no colonial structural attraction, but the works of art cover most continents and many centuries, including Rubens and Goya originals.

TAKE ME OUT TO THE BALLGAME

In a 1999 home-and-away series, the Baltimore Orioles traveled to Cuba and defeated a Cuban national team without many of its star players (who at the time were involved in the Cuban league's playoff finals) by the score of 3–2 in 11 innings. In a show of solidarity, Orioles star first baseman Will Clark took a case of beer to the Cubans' bus. The Cubans then traveled to Baltimore, where they trounced the Orioles 12–6 in a historic athletic exchange, the first time in history that a Cuban team had played a U.S. major league squad in the United States. This was also the first time in the history of sports that a team with a total annual player payroll of US$2,000 defeated another team whose total team payroll was US$78 million.

By inviting the Cubans, Orioles owner Peter Angelos had made a statement against the embargo, and as expected, he and his team were met at the stadium by Cuban exile protesters, several of whom ran onto the field with anti-Castro signs.

On Washington, D.C. radio, a popular sportscaster was told by a Cuban exile that Peter Angelos' cavorting with Cubans was like a Jew embracing Hitler. What the sportscaster did not know was that after the revolution's prohibition of private enterprise, Fidel Castro made an exception for Jewish butchers so that religious Jews could maintain their kosher diet. Nor was the sportscaster aware that the death squads and torture so prevalent in

173

other Latin American regimes supported by the U.S. government and extremist Cuban exile groups were nonexistent in Cuba. Yes, Cuba had its human rights violations, but the comparison with Hitler was a most creative example of historical revisionism. The sportscaster remained mute before his guest's accusations.

The visiting Cubans knew that they would be totally outnumbered in the media by their influential exile brethren but nevertheless considered this sports diplomacy of the utmost symbolic importance, since baseball is Cuba's national pastime.

Whether or not you understand baseball, a visit to the **Estadio Latinoamericano** in Cerro during the baseball season between November and March is a must for anyone who wishes to immerse themselves in Cuban culture.

This ain't Brooklyn . . . just your typical Havana streetball game.

The Estadio Latinoamericano.

Cuba's baseball culture dates back to the 19th century, and like Havana's 1950s Chevys, baseball history seems to have frozen at a time when teams where "clubs" and players maintained an allegiance to their neighborhood and city. More than the modern, impersonal type of "entertainment," attending a Cuban baseball game is a civic event. The players usually work as physical education teachers in local schools and are known personally by the children and adult neighbors.

The Estadio Latinoamericano is a brisk walk from Centro Habana or may be reached by bus from Parque de la Fraternidad. Local newspapers will announce the times and places for other spectator sports events like basketball, volleyball, and track and field. Visitors interested in joining in are usually welcomed into pickup stickball, punchball, basketball, and handball games, at local parks or in the streets.

BEACHES

The Bay of Havana's patron saint, Yemayá, syncretized with the Virgin of Regla, will guide you to the sea, dressed in blues and whites (blue for the sea, white for the sands on the beach). Yemayá, Yoruba mistress of the seas.

The closest beaches west of urban Havana are in **Miramar** and **Playa de Marianao**. Beach purists will find the rocks and crowds of people disturbing, especially during the summer months, but the lively ambiance (people singing around guitarists and bongo players, beach volleyball games, etc.) is the main compensating factor. At the other end of Havana, past the exclusive tourist resorts of **Playas del Este** are the beaches within two blocks of the main street that crosses through Guanabo. **Guanabo** is an independent community that is technically part of Havana, with its own restaurants, *paladares*, farmers' markets, attractive but inexpensive hotels, and homestays, all within beachcombing distance of the more idyllic **Brisas del Mar** to the east.

The best way to reach the beach from within the city is by sharing a taxi. Beaches to the west are also reached via buses departing from Parque de la Fraternidad in Centro Habana, and to the east, by buses from near the Estación Central, which also sends trains to Playas del Este during the summer.

NIGHTCLUBS

For this writer, Havana's local neighborhood taverns and restaurants with their roving musicians are more pleasurable than fancy nightclubs where your neighbors, for economic reasons, will never show up. Every large hotel has its nightclub, most of which require reservations. If you had one to chose, perhaps the **Parisien** cabaret has the most to offer. The show is generous, prices are half what you'd pay at the Tropicana, and the hotel itself, on a hill overlooking the ocean from Vedado, is a relic of nostalgia from Batista times.

The beaches near Guanabo.

If you time it right, a visit to **Palacio de la Salsa**, in the nearby Riviera, can bring you up close to one of Cuba's internationally acclaimed salsa bands like **Los Van Van**. Prices are steep, and if you've got time in Havana, sooner or later you'll hear the same band at a street festival.

Smaller, more intimate cabarets are beginning to sprout up. For a fraction of the price, Cuban music (especially salsa, *son*, bolero, or Latin jazz) is found in Old Havana bars and restaurants during daytime hours. You get what you hear, so listen from the outside first to make sure this is the kind of music you've been waiting for. Some of Cuba's best musicians arrive unannounced and play in funky surroundings reminiscent of Mississippi Delta juke joints. Word of mouth is the best way to find these events, which often occur on Sunday afternoons and into the evening.

Son is an exciting, Afro-Hispanic music with African rhythms and call-and-response vocal patterns originating in the Oriente of Cuba. (Look for the music of Cuban *son* virtuoso **Compay Segundo**.) Rumba is an urban percussion-chorus music originating on the streets of Matanzas and Havana. (Listen to **Los Muñequitos de Matanzas**.) Salsa developed when Cubans who had experienced New York jazz in the 1940s added brass instruments to *son* bands. (Dance to Los Van Van, **NG La Banda**, **Isaac Delgado**, or **Irakere**.)

PARKS

One Cuban-American remarked to me that Havana was a culturally-deprived city because it lacked theme parks. He was right. There are no theme parks in the whole city. Disney is absent.

Instead, there are extensive green areas that offer the best of the tropics and are still located close to the urban density of Havana's center. These romantic havens are reached by either bicycle, bus, or taxi. The most rewarding way to visit Havana's huge parks is by bicycle. Bikes can be rented at most hotels; a long-stay visitor might want to simply take apart his bicycle and bring it to Havana.

Jardín Botánica Nacional, in Arroyo Naranjo, with its US$3 entrance fee, contains trees and flowers from North and South America, Africa, and Oceania, as well as a traditional Japanese garden. (Disobeying U.S. travel restrictions are various plants native to the United States.) Within just 2.3 square miles (6 square km), there are some 140,000 varieties of plants, including more than 500 different types of orchids and more than 1,000 types of cactus which no doubt are thirsting for more arid climates. An organic vegetarian restaurant (lunch-hour only) serves food grown on the premises.

El Bosque de la Habana is a jungle within the city, whose Almendares River is being cleaned and restored through a major municipal program that includes ecological brigades of children from nearby schools. Enter from Nuevo Vedado.

Havana has two zoos. **Parque Zoológico Nacional**, located in a suburb 2 miles (3 km) from the city, is home to giraffes, hippos, antelopes, zebras, and rhinos roaming freely. Microbuses take you through the animal park, or you can watch the wild animals from a restaurant on a hill overlooking the action. There's also an area where children can pet the baby animals. How they were able to feed all this wildlife during the Special Period remains a mystery. I asked a zoo guide if the survival of these great big animals was somehow related to the lack of stray dogs on the streets of Havana. I got a smile in return. The other zoo, **Parque Zoológico de la Habana** (located on 26th Avenue in Nuevo Vedado) adds to the impressive green areas of the city and is adjacent to the Bosque de la Habana.

Parque Lenin in Arroyo Naranjo offers an amphitheater overlooking a fish pool, an art gallery, a ceramics workshop, literary readings, children's theater, horseback riding, swimming pools, and a small train that does the circuit of the park. A restaurant called **Las Ruinas** was built upon the colonial ruins of an old sugar factory.

Last but not least of the larger Havana parks is the **Cementerio Cristóbal Colón**, whose Santería caretaker is Oyá, mistress of the winds and queen of the cemetery. Located in Nuevo Vedado, Cementerio Cristóbal Colón lies halfway between the bus terminal and the Almendares River. Inaugurated in the second half of the 19th century, this cemetery doubles as a sculpture and architectural garden with an idyllic setting. Within the chapel at the center of the cemetery is a fresco called "El Purgatorio," an example of 19th century Cuban painting.

SIDE TRIPS OUTSIDE OF HAVANA

Most visitors to Havana also visit the waterfalls in Soroa; the unearthly, flat-topped *mogotes* in the tobacco growing valley of Viñales; the classic colonial town (and rumba center of the world) in Matanzas; and the white beaches of Varadero (Cuba's version of Cancún). You'll have a great time in all these places. But here we offer one of the best-kept side-trip secrets. It's the small city of **Cárdenas**, and it's only 9 miles (15 km) east of Varadero.

Time Travel in Cárdenas

Havana's colonial arcades and vintage cars look like Star Trek futurism compared to the setting in Cárdenas. Forget the 1949 Fords. Here, the only form of private transportation is the bicycle. Forget the *camellos*. Here, the only form of public transportation is the horse-and-buggy (called a *coche* in Cárdenas), with a fare of one peso. At the nearby sugar plantation, a 1888 steam engine hails sugar to port. Michael Jordan could pass through the tall doorways of this city's colonial buildings without bumping his head, and if he leaped, his outstretched arms would not reach the ceiling.

This time warp has nothing to do with the special period. "They've always lived this way," says Iván, a Havana resident who loves to visit Cárdenas. It only costs him 6 Cuban pesos by bus from Havana (US$6 for foreigners) for the three-hour ride covering about 81 miles (130 km), but he can get there faster on his motorcycle. "It's refreshing to travel from the 19th century modernism of El Prado in Havana to the laid-back 17th century of Cárdenas," he explains.

The only factor distorting this time warp is the people, who talk and act like citizens of the 20th century, although it never dawns on them that there could be a better form of transportation than the horse-and-buggy. Even a Cuban air force pilot from Cárdenas hops on a horse-and-buggy as if it were the right way to go.

The best restaurant in town is **Cafe Espriu**, right on Plaza Echevarría. Few tourists visit this city, so you wonder how this place, with about a US$2 mean charge, can thrive. You discover that Cárdenas is a relatively prosperous town, in spite of the fact that its public transportation system is fueled by hay. Many residents work in the tourist industry in nearby Varadero.

Cárdenas has several music-and-dance restaurants on the main street, **Avenida Céspedes**, and on the same avenue, a cozy art gallery called **Salón Massaguer**, with varied styles including art naif, surrealism, expressionism, and socialist realism.

Nearby is the public market, where you should say hello to my friend Jorge Luis, who sells the best onions in town. Since so few visitors show up in Cárdenas, there are no formal bicycle rental places, so you have to make friends and then lending arrangements with the locals. You can bike in one direction to the seaport, where an old rum factory still operates, or in the other direction to the zoo, and past that to the Central Azucarero José Smith Comás to see the 1888 steam engine mentioned previously.

Lodging

One can stay at the town's only hotel, **Hotel Dominique**, with a huge room with a view of Avenida Céspedes. Or you can visit the **Dirección Municipal de Vivienda** on Laborde #518 (tel: 52-2852),

181

where a friendly woman by the name of Lanexys will help you find a homestay.

Getting There

From Havana's central bus terminal (near Plaza de la Revolución), a bus trip to Cárdenas for foreigners costs US$6, but for your return, they have no choice but to sell you the same ticket for 6 Cuban pesos because they don't deal in *divisa* (dollars). Only one bus goes to Cárdenas each day, leaving about 9:00 am, and returning to Havana about 1:00 p.m., thus requiring an overnight stay. You must arrive an hour early to get your reserved ticket in a blue office to the right of the entrance to the Havana bus terminal. Hustler drivers parked outside will offer you a faster trip via collective taxi for about US$15, depending on how many customers they've roped in.

Orientation

Cárdenas's Eiffel Tower, a tall TV antenna, stands just off Céspedes Avenue and is a perfect central landmark that makes it impossible for you to get lost. There are no high-rise view blockers. The farmers' market is two blocks to the west of the tower, and Plaza Echevarría, with the cafe and the city's two eclectic museums, is two blocks to the east.

Other Trip Tips

Travelers to the *mogote* mountain region in **Viñales** would do best to hire a car and divide the costs among the group. There are plenty of caves to be explored, and if you go with a formal tour, they don't leave you time for exploring. Hikers should use mosquito repellent.

Travelers to **Matanzas** should schedule their trips according to music preferences. Wednesday nights are free symphony orchestra concerts and Fridays and Saturdays have various salsa and rumba alternatives, the most atmospheric of which is nicknamed **La Ruina**, a stonewalled restaurant built from the ruins of an old sugar factory. The 4:50 p.m. LADIS train to Matanzas from La Estación Central is comfortable even if it looks like pre-restoration Old Havana on wheels.

Don't expect tips here about **Varadero**, which is off-limits to most Cubans and looks like any other resort. The white sands are soft, the emerald sea is seductive, it's a beautiful place, and any tour agent can get you there.

As long as Cuba has a fuel shortage, policemen called *amarillos* will be stationed under highway bridges to flag down government and private vehicles to pick up passengers. This system is not recommended for visitors to Cuba, since you'll be taking rides away from Cubans who need them more than you do. I do know of one shoestring traveler from Argentina who got around the whole country thanks to the *amarillos*.

ADDENDA: ENTERTAINMENT VENUES

These days, the entertainment industry revolves around the celebrity industry. Concerts in stadiums where you need binoculars to see the entertainers replace music clubs where the musicians sit and chat amongst the active listeners. Millionaire professional athletes advertising Nike or Coca Cola and shifting allegiance to sports teams that bid the highest salaries replace members of local sports clubs who share the same community with their spectators. Some Cuban baseball players have decided that the wealth of celebrityhood is irresistible and sign a contract a with Major League baseball team. But the majority still travel abroad, defeat the Baltimore Orioles, and then return to their hometown communities to teach physical education.

A few select Cuban salsa and jazz performers have been handed a ticket to the celebrity fraternity abroad (e.g., Los Van Van and Gonzalo Rubalcaba) as they travel to Europe or North America to perform. But somehow, these artists manage to take the personalized and humanized style of Cuban entertainment with them, and the difference is deeply felt. You dance to Los Van Van in Paris or San Francisco, and you go up between sets and shake their hands.

Theme parks celebrate with nostalgia the sense of history and community that they have replaced. In Orlando, Florida there is a theme park with a fake scenario imitating the exciting city of Key West. Once the trade embargo is lifted, someone will surely conjure up a theme park that imitates the Malecón and Old Havana. Or if the market economy floods in and speculators are given free reign, Old Havana itself could become an outdoor theme park, resembling certain gentrified districts of Paris. Today's thriving tourist industry in Cuba has effectively removed a few "entertainment" venues from their communities and conjured up imitations of the depersonalized type of entertainment one finds abroad. Yet Havana's relative isolation from the global economy has served to protect most of its stadiums, theaters, dance halls, and music clubs from the disenfranchisement of the entertainment industry.

Music Venues

At **Casa de la trova**, San Lázaro, between Gervasio and Belascoán, and other houses like it, you can hear *la trova cubana*, which contrary to popular belief, existed as bolero, *punto cubano* and other genres long before revolutionary singer-poets like Pablo Milanés and Silvio Rodríguez catapulted to international fame. Everyone still knows them as Silvio and Pablo. Their Cuban roots are complemented by the influence of the Catalán *cantoautor*, Joan Manuel Serrat.

Other peso music venues include **Palmares** (Malecón and E, in Vedado), **Holá Ola**, the **Malecón**, and live band settings in hotels like the **Caribbean** and **Nueva York**, near El Prado.

"Straight ahead" jazz is not as widely popular in Cuba as one would expect, since salsa itself incorporates jazz rhythms and harmonies. The **Coparrun** (in the Hotel Riviera) and **El Zorro y el Cuevo** (23 and O in Vedado) are U.S. dollar venues with jazz groups. Ask around for other venues not known specifically as jazz clubs but which offer jazz on particular nights of the week.

Rumba groups like Los Muñequitos de Matanzas are incredibly popular and yet maintain their roots at the level of the common people. They often arrive without fanfare and fill local lofts with energetic crowds through word of mouth, with admission for 10 or 20 pesos (US$0.50 or US$1). I was asking for Los Muñequitos one Sunday afternoon in Centro Habana and a group of people said, "They're playing today, come on with us," and they took me by the arm.

Check daily editions of *Granma* for the week's events, with locations and times listed. More adventurous is to go club hunting. Start with a stroll along Calzada in Vedado, between Paseo and Avenida de los Presidentes.

Theater and Dance Venues

Gran Teatro de la Habana, across from Parque Central, is a collectors' item flashing seductive baroque architecture. For less than a dollar, you may see a performance by a new theater company, any of the country's contemporary dance groups, or Cuba's world famous folk group, Conjunto Folklórico Nacional. **Teatro Karl Marx** (Av 1 near the Malecón at 10 in Miramar) may offer an exciting surprise with one of several international prize winning theater groups or an avant-garde theater company.

A dance experience you don't want to miss is the legendary **Ballet Nacional de Cuba**, which has become a Havana icon under the artistic direction of Alicia Alonso. This is Cuba's version of Bolshoi, with a repertory that includes classical, folk and modern dance. Having performed successfully in New York, Ms. Alonso could have become a U.S. celebrity, but instead she remained in Cuba. Her ballet troupe accumulates thousands of frequent flyer miles every year, and by chance may be performing in your country when you are in Havana.

Vedado is Havana's theater district. For more adventurous theater experiences, take a chance on smaller theaters like **Guiñot** (19 at M), **Bertolt Brecht** (13 and I), **Mella** (Línea at A), and **Hubert de Blanck** (Calzada at A).

CHAPTER TEN

MENU OF EVENTS:
Festivals, -ologies, and Everything in Between

Havana's menu of special events differs from that of other Latin American capitals in its primarily secular agenda. Festivals in most cities of Latin America are based on Hispanic Catholic religious traditions, often with a blend of indigenous religious customs. Even before the Cuban Revolution, the Catholic religion was not a dominant force in society. For a majority of Cubans, there was the image of the Church using its influence to prolong the Spanish colony long after most other Latin American countries had won their independence. Unable to pay for baptisms and communions, poorer Cubans had drifted away from the Church long before the 1959 Revolution, when the society was secularized.

Even after the Pope's visit to Cuba in 1998 and the new humanitarian role of what is left of the Church, most Havana festivals were of a nonreligious nature, with Afro-Cuban Santería beliefs surfacing as the most obvious religious component. In recognition of this religious preference, Cuban authorities invited African religious figures prior to the Pope's visit.

Even without any annual festivals, Havana would still be a festive city. The spontaneous nature of Havana festivities, breaking out on any day or at any hour, to a certain extent replaces the annual event as the mainstay of city life.

HOLIDAYS AND FESTIVALS

Carnaval

Havana's most important festival of religious heritage is Carnaval, which is held on weekend evenings in front of the Capitolio and at other historic venues in the city during a period that parallels the February Carnaval of Brazil or New Orleans. Dancing groups called *comparsas* are accompanied by conga percussionists and trumpets, with rumba dancers waving lanterns and choruses singing praise to the Yoruban saints, or *orishas*, each of whom has a Catholic equivalent.

Santería Celebrations

Knowledge of a few important *orishas* will enhance appreciation of neighborhood religious festivals. The names of these African gods/saints pop up in salsa and rumba tunes constantly. Obatalá, dressed in white, is the god of peace, justice and wisdom. Yemayá, syncretized with the Virgin of Regla, is the patron saint of the bay and the sea, dressed in blue and white. (Make sure to be in the district of Regla, a five-minute ferry ride across the bay from Old Havana, on September 7, when a procession venerating Yemayá winds through the streets).

This cigar-smoking Santería believer will read your fortune in the name of Yemayá.

Oggún, the equivalent of St. Peter, is the god of war. His brother, Changó, dressed in red, is the equivalent of St. Barbara and worshipped as the lord of fire, thunder, and virility. Ochán (Our Lady of Charity), sister of Yemayá and dressed in yellow, is the sensorial *orisha* of rivers, lakes, and eroticism. Oyá, in multicolored dress, is the queen of lightning and the cemetery. Olofi, the supreme creator, strangely keeps a lower profile than many of the other *orishas*. Santería priests, called *babalawos*, operate out of their apartments, giving useful advice to believers through a complex system of divination based on seashells, stones, and other artifacts.

Santería is referred to by some insiders as Regla de Ocha (Rule of the Gods). Aside from the dominant Yoruba version of Santería, there are other smaller sects such as Palo Monte and Abakuá (of which musician Chano Pozo was a distinguished ad-

189

herent). The syncretism of African gods with Catholic saints developed in the slavery era, when Catholic officials repressed manifestations of African religions. Slaves responded by hiding their faith by appearing to worship Catholic saints, from which the word Santería is derived.

Although not on any agenda of religious festivals, Santería celebrations maintain their tradition. By word of mouth, visitors will learn the when and where of these events.

Secular Festivals

One of Havana's biggest secular festivals is the **Havana International Jazz Festival**, which is scheduled during the winter. The **International Guitar Festival** (May), the **International Theater Festival** (August or September), the **International Ballet Festival** (October), and the **International Latin American Film Festival** (December) had all been postponed or reduced to biannual affairs during the Special Period, but as the economic situation continues to improve, most will return to their annual status.

A two-hour train trip to nearby Matanzas is a must for festival lovers; beginning October 10 and lasting a week-and-a-half is the **Festival del Bailador Rumbero**, a wild rumba happening in and around the 1862 neoclassical Teatro Sauto, in the city where the rumba was born.

National Holidays
National Cuban holidays include **Liberation Day** (the anniversary of the triumph of the Revolution on January 1, 1959), **May Day** (May 1, in remembrance of the Haymarket Square "Martyrs of Chicago" labor demonstration, which became the international labor day in every country but the one where it originated), **National Rebellion Day** (the anniversary of the initiation of the Cuban Revolution on July 26, 1953), and the **Anniversary of the Wars of Independence** (which celebrates the rebellion started by Cuban revolutionary hero Carlos Manuel de Céspedes on October 10, 1868).

HAVANA: THE "-OLOGY" CAPITAL OF THE WORLD
On the surface, it makes no sense. Here's a tropical island where the people dance to salsa, play baseball, and produce things like cigars, rum, and sugar. It has all the ingredients of a sweet, after-dinner, dessert type of place, not a heavy main-course culture. Anyone deceived by geographical determinism might link Cuba with the tropics mystique, a place to exercise or relax the body, not to expand the mind. We inherit these stereotypes from the post-colonial era. We are conditioned to know, for sure, that the world's intellectual advances come from places with temperate climates. The tropics are for providing raw materials and for relaxing on the beach.

Since 1959, Cuba has defied such stereotypes and made its largest city, Havana, an intellectual capital of the world. The prevailing wisdom of Cuban ideologues was to prioritize the development of human resources, expecting that the rest would fall into place. For this reason, Cuba pours an enormous percentage of its budget into education, culture, and scientific research.

Conference-aholics Get Ready . . .

Anyone from abroad who works in a field that ends in "-ology" (or any related profession) is likely to find the Havana conference of his choice. And we're not only talking about marine biology or hurricane meteorology. Theologists of all faiths, for example, seem to find a haven for religious conferences in this largely secular country.

Cuba's extensive international conference schedule can be divided into two basic categories. Category One includes events that relate to Cuba's immediate geographical, historical or cultural reality, such as **FolkCuba**, the **José Martí Colloquium**, the **Benny Moré Popular Music Festival**, **African Roots of Cuban Culture**, and **Cubadanza**. Within this category are also cultural and intellectual events obviously associated with advances of the Cuban Revolution, in fields like ballet, sports, medicine, education, and filmmaking. Examples include **Cuballet**, the **Havana Film Festival**, the **International Hemingway Conference**, the **Primary Health Care Conference**, and the **Advanced Techniques on Clinical Neurophysiology Symposium**. Other areas of less-publicized development in Cuba have their own conferences— **Geriatrics**, **Engineering and Architecture**, the **International Academy of Law and Mental Health** (Havana is famous for its humane and creatively therapeutic psychiatric hospital), **Historic Preservation and Sustainable Development**, a cultural patrimony conference, and a variety of environmentalist conferences.

Category Two of the Havana conference list includes the most incongruous events. A country that has to hire a visiting rabbi for Jewish high holidays receives an inordinate number of

Jewish groups for international seminars. Havana's secular environment seems conducive to groups of other faiths and denominations as well, like the **McAtee Religious Delegation**, the **New Orleans Presbyterian Church**, the **Disciples of Christ**, the **Columbia Theological Seminary**, and the **Cuban Evangelical Celebration**.

A country that is the object of a trade embargo by the United States receives university study groups from across the United States (a few among them being: **American University**, the **City University of New York Law School**, **Colorado College**, **Drake University**, **Texas A&M**, the **University of Illinois**, **Virginia Tech**, and **Westminster College**, which chose Cuba as the appropriate site to experience the change of the millennium). Embargo or no embargo, the **Conference of North American and Cuban Philosophers and Social Scientists** has already met eleven times in Havana. A country not known as a vanguard in private enterprise hosts the **University of North Carolina Business School**.

The list goes on. A country that is supposed to be repressive holds a criminology congress for law enforcement agents seeking more humane ways to apply the law. A country where salsa was born is unexpectedly the host of international events on classical and contemporary orchestral music.

The story of how Cuba has been able to expand its offerings as a cultural and intellectual center of the world, even when confronting the mid-1990s economic hardships, goes far beyond the aggressive promotion of events. To pull it off, there has to be a cultural infrastructure and a national commitment for such events.

Case Study:
The Sala de Conciertos José White de Matanzas

I asked Everaldo Carbonell, Artistic Director of the Sala de Conciertos, how a small city like Matanzas, a cultural satellite of Havana, could maintain a regular program of cultural events.

193

"More than 140 years ago, we had a literary and artistic high school in this building [on the north side of Parque Libertad]. In 1959, what was the National Sports Institute became the Casa de Cultura Provincial. There was a concerted attempt to bring culture to all the people."

The Sala de Conciertos of Matanzas changed its name several times along the way, until it acquired its present name, in remembrance of the 19th century violinist José White.

As I listened to the Tuesday morning symphony orchestra rehearsal, I asked Mr. Carbonell how he could finance Tuesday evening literary readings, Wednesday evening orchestra concerts, and weekend events as well.

"Concert music is financially protected by the Cuban government," he explained. "There's free admission to our Wednesday concerts and other events. And our orchestra changes its repertory each week, so the required rehearsal time would not be available were it not for government support."

Smaller Cuban cities and towns all have their cultural centers. Local talent is discovered, and local artists who become distinguished in their regions are given the chance to study in Havana. This was the case of 21-year-old Giselle Grau Garcells, from Holguín, who was winning provincial awards for her piano playing since the age of ten. The cultural infrastructure of the provinces like Holguín helped develop talent that would have been lost in countries where rural areas are abandoned by the State. After concerts and awards in Italy, Mexico, and South America, Giselle came to Havana to study with the great Cuban classical and jazz pianist Andrés Alén.

In this way, the cultural infrastructure of provincial Cuba provides a meaningful context for enriching Havana's development in the arts and sciences. Havana could not have become an international center of culture and intellectual life had it not been for a nationwide effort to support the arts and sciences, as exem-

An "-ology" conference landmark of Havana: the imposing Capitolio, home of the Cuban Academy of Sciences.

195

plified by the government-subsidized Sala de Conciertos in Matanzas.

Before going to Cuba, pick up a calendar with a schedule of main events in the arts, sciences, and academia from your local travel agent specializing in Cuba. Such a list is available internationally from **Marazul Tours**, located at Tower Plaza, 4100 Park Ave, Weehawken, NJ 07087, USA (fax: 201-319-9009; web site: *http://www.marazultours.com*). For more specific events that may not be included within a general calendar, scholars and researchers should consult their particular professional association. This is how my friend from India, Dr. Biranda Das, became a participant in a Havana conference on nuclear medicine.

The setting for conferences of the '-ologists' is usually in one of Old or Centro Habana's more aesthetically appealing historic buildings, including the Capitolio. Cuban intellectuals have done their best to make you oblivious to what's happening outside the conference center, on the Malecón, in the plazas, on the beach, and at rumba get-togethers.

POSTSCRIPT: LEAVING HAVANA

The psychological void felt by Havana visitors as they await their flight to their home country is a pervasive mood among most of us who have been forever touched by the contagion of this exciting and emotionally gripping city. In the waiting area of the colorful José Martí International Airport, people clutching their boarding passes are plotting their next visit to Havana, already missing the great friends they've made.

By the time Ernest Hemingway had settled in Cuba, he'd already written his *A Moveable Feast* about Paris. But long after Paris was a distant memory, Hemingway had adopted Havana as his expatriate home. Upon departing, we need to pack, within our emotional luggage, the right tools to maintain the flame of our Havana experience aglow until our next visit. Trinkets and photographs will not do. We need something more substantial, our own moveable feast.

Foremost is a directory of our Havana friends. Mail to Cuba is slow and undependable. Those letters that do arrive may take up to six weeks. One letter from Cuba arrived to me after three months. The most effective way to send letters to Cuba is by certifying with a return coupon. The extra investment is worth it. Since I've used this strategy, 100 percent of my letters to Cuba have arrived! An alternative is electronic mail. Some of your Cuban friends may have their own e-mail address at their location of employment. In an emergency, the courier who knows Havana the best is DHL.

It is said that among the senses, the strongest conveyor of memories is the sense of smell. Smokers have it easy within this realm of the senses as they can pack Cuban cigars and reexperience Havana by recreating Cohiba and Montecristo aromas on their own front porch. Otherwise, while you're in Cuba, try to watch Cuban cooks, and learn how they use garlic. Then create a typical Cuban aroma in your own kitchen.

But among the senses, the sense of sound is Havana's greatest asset. Even more than a camera, a tape recorder is the medium that best captures Havana's complex, sensorial rhythms. Music (rumba, *son*, salsa, bolero and *trova*) is the most obvious target for our tape recorder. But the daily life of Havana is music itself, the groan of a 1949 Ford starting up in the sweet morning, the slurping of the waves against the Malecón, and above all the mellow, rhythmic sing-song of flirting Cuban voices.

And when you're home with time for meditation, you can listen to Los Van Van, NG La Banda, Isaac Delgado or Irakere, and ask the nearest mate, husband-wife, boyfriend-girlfriend, daughter-son, or a total stranger, to dance to the rhythms of salsa, rumba and *son*.

197

BIBLIOGRAPHY

Hundreds of books and articles have been scrutinized in order to research the controversial theme of this book. Every time I thought I'd found a truth, an opposite truth would emerge from a separate source. This is not a statistical book, but many of the concepts herein were the result of an accumulation of apparently reliable statistics. My extensive bibliography reflects an honest attempt to unravel distortions created around the theme of Cuba. A few of the most startling, informative, and useful sources are cited here.

American Association for World Health. *The Impact of the U.S. Embargo on Health & Nutrition in Cuba: Denial of Food and Medicine.* Washington, D.C., 1997. A thorough study, loaded with objective facts and figures on Cuba's health care system and the impact of the U.S. trade embargo.

Alfonso Hernández, Carmen R. *100 preguntas y respuestas sobre Cuba* (100 questions and answers about Cuba). Havana: Editorial Pablo de la Torriente, 1996. An official panorama of contemporary Cuba.

Annual reports of Amnesty International, 1997 and 1998. Amnesty International is a prestigious, nonpolitical organization. It has documented the existence of political prisoners and "prisoners of conscience" in Cuba. Cuban authorities claim these prisoners were working to overthrow the State and thus engaged in sedition. Citing the existence of Puerto Rican, Native American and Black Panther long-term political prisoners in the United States, they claim the U.S. lacks the moral authority to stand in judgment of Cuba. Cuba also interprets human rights as economic justice, and believes that its admirable record in health care, education, and economic equality should be considered within the realm of human rights.

Burgos, Tomás. Poetry with a personal interpretation of Santería, appearing in various publications. Burgos is also a scientist with published papers and seminar presentations.

Cameron, Sarah. *Cuba Handbook*. Bath: Footprint Books, 1998. Co-published in the U.S. by Passport Books. The author is a specialist on Latin America, and her historical and cultural introductions are concise yet insightful. Some of the info in the edition mentioned is outdated, but an updated version is now available.

Castañeda, Jorge G. *The Life and Death of Che Guevara*. New York: Alfred F. Knopf, 1998.

Covert Action Quarterly, no. 65 (Fall 1998). (Web site: *http://www.covertaction.org*). Several articles from an independent leftist perspective on Cuban reality.

Granma Internacional (March 1999) carries one article on the ecological restoration of Havana's Almendares River, and a short history of Cuban food. *Granma*, the organ of the Cuban Communist Party, used to be heavy on political rhetoric, but today's *Granma* carries a larger proportion of cultural articles (web site: *http://www.granma.cu*).

The Guardian. Numerous *Guardian* articles have been consulted. *Guardian* stringers in Cuba are an excellent source of information and do not represent a single point of view. Check *Guardian* files under "Cuba" in U.K. libraries.

Hamstra, Mark. "Cuba is eyed as a potential expansion frontier," *Nation's Restaurant News* (June 16, 1997), p. 18.

"The Island of Dr. Castro," *U.S. News & World Report* (May 5, 1997), pp. 39–43. Concrete information on Cuba's advances in biotechnology, with an informative sidebar on health tourism.

Kurlansky, Mark. "Havana 1990s: the Babalawos and the Birds," *The Reader's Companion to Cuba*. New York: Harcourt Brace, 1997. This is the most engaging account of a foreigner interacting with Havana's Santerían religious scene.

Leal Spengler, Eusebio. *Viaje en la memoria* (A voyage in memory). Havana: Oficina del Historiador de la Ciudad de la Habana, 1996. A philosophical and visionary narration about the plans for the restoration of Old Havana, with maps and impressive color photos.

Oldenburg, Ray. *The Great Good Place*. New York: Paragon House, 1991. There is nothing about Havana in this book by one of the foremost urbanologists in the United States. However, the author provides a perceptive theoretical framework for understanding Havana's street-life.

Ortiz, Fernando. *Los tambores batá de los yorubas* (The Batá Drums of the Yorubas) and *Poesía y canto de los negros afrocubanos* (Poetry and Song of Black Afro-Cubans). Havana: Publicigraf, 1994. Ortiz is a musicologist and ethnologist; these books are for readers who want to understand the details of the Yoruba/Afro-Cuban experience. Both titles are available for a couple of Cuban pesos in Havana's new and used bookstores.

"Paraíso perdido" (Paradise lost), *Newsweek en español* (July 2, 1997), pp. 16–20. A spicy but objective look at Havana's survival mode during the "special period," with color photos of award-winning quality.

Rice, John. "Cuba Cracks Down on Crime, Hustling," *Associated Press* (January 23, 1999). Mr. Rice missed some of the hustlers who still find a way of operating in spite of the police crackdown. Nevertheless, this short article is a fair and interesting presentation of Cuba's reality at the street level.

Rosado, Alfredo. "Vivir en Cuba" (Living in Cuba), *Contenido* (November, 1998), pp. 38–43. *Contenido* is a Mexican magazine for a popular audience. The author distinguishes between Cuba's *jineteras* and traditional prostitution, interpreting Cuba's sexual reality with subtle nuances.

Rosset, Peter and Benjamin Medea. *The Greening of the Revolution: Cuba's Experiment with Organic Agriculture*. Melbourne: Ocean

Press, 1994. Co-published by Global Exchange in San Francisco. This book is still very enlightening about food customs, and the dramatic historical process that led to today's thriving *agromercados*.

Scheer, Robert. "On Cuba, JFK Was Married to the Mob: Hersh's revelations, from poison cigars to infected pills, were reported by the CIA itself," *Los Angeles Times* (November 11, 1997).

Schroth, Raymond A. "Cuba sinks under weight of Fidel's dated phobias," *National Catholic Reporter* (September 5, 1997), pp. 10–11.

Segre, Roberto, Mario Coyula, and Joseph L. Scarpaci. *Havana: Two Faces of the Antillean Metropolis*. New York: John Wiley & Sons, 1997. You lose some of the thrills of the city with the encyclopedic approach of this book, but it is still informative and visionary.

U.N. Human Development Report, 1998. The best source for comparative statistics on quality of life in various countries. Within the report is the "Human Poverty Index," which, based on indicators related to health, education, sanitation, and diet, names Cuba as second best among the world's poor countries. When personal income is factored in to the "Human Development Index," Cuba finishes in the middle of the pack.

Waitzkin, Howard. "Primary Care in Cuba: Low- and High-technology Developments," *Journal of Family Practice* (September 1997), pp. 250–259.

Weissman, Steve. "How Fidel Got His Billions," *Feature News International* (1998). A former TV producer for the BBC, Steve Weissman is a widely published journalist and an expert on Cuba. By the same author: "My Cuban Problem—and Ours," *Tikkun* (September 1997), pp. 69–72.

THE AUTHOR

Mark Cramer triangulates his life between New York City, La Paz, and, currently, Paris (thus obligating his son Marcus to learn three languages by the age of ten). His favorite cities in the world are Paris, New York, Havana, Barcelona, and San Francisco — not necessarily in that order.

Cramer has written books on Bolivia, Mexico, Cuba, California, and New York for the *Culture Shock!* travel series. His *Funky Towns USA: The Best Alternative, Eclectic, and Visionary Places* (1995) was featured on CNN, written up in more than 50 newspapers and journals, and is now used as a text at several universities. Author and urbanologist Ray Oldenburg calls Mark Cramer "a seasoned expert in urban anatomy."

INDEX